ELEARNING

Elearning has long been touted as the brave new frontier of education, offering new challenges to teachers, students and, indeed, the whole of the education system. This timely book is the perfect reference for anyone seeking to navigate the myriad of names, concepts and applications associated with this new era of teaching, training and learning.

Elearning: The Key Concepts takes you from A to Z through a range of topics, including:

- Blogging
- Course design
- Plagiarism
- Search engines
- Self-directed learning
- Tutoring
- Virtual Learning Environments (VLEs)

Fully cross-referenced, the book also includes a substantial introduction exploring the development of elearning and putting these new challenges in context, and provides extensive suggestions for further reading, making this an invaluable guide to a vital field.

Professor Robin Mason is a specialist in the research and practice of online teaching and learning at the Open University. **Dr Frank Rennie** is Head of Research and Postgraduate Development at Lews Castle College, the University of Highlands and Islands Millennium Institute.

Also available from Routledge

Internet: The Basics
John Whittaker
0–415–25746–8

Cyberculture: The Key Concepts
David J. Bell, Brian Loader, Nicholas Pleace and Douglas Schuler
0–415–24754–3

Secondary Education: The Key Concepts
Jerry Wellington
0–415–34404–2

Fifty Major Thinkers on Education
Edited by Joy Palmer
Advisory Editors: Liora Bresler and David E. Cooper
0–415–23126–4

Fifty Modern Thinkers on Education
Edited by Joy Palmer
Advisory Editors: Liora Bresler and David E. Cooper
0–415–22409–8

ELEARNING

The Key Concepts

Robin Mason and Frank Rennie

Routledge
Taylor & Francis Group

LONDON AND NEW YORK

First published 2006
by Routledge
2 Park Square, Milton Park, Abingdon, Oxon OX14 4RN

Simultaneously published in the USA and Canada
by Routledge
270 Madison Ave, New York, NY 10016

Routledge is an imprint of the Taylor & Francis Group, an informa business

© 2006 Robin Mason and Frank Rennie

Typeset in Bembo by
RefineCatch Limited, Bungay, Suffolk
Printed and bound in Great Britain by
MPG Books Ltd, Bodmin

British Library Cataloguing in Publication Data
A catalogue record for this book is available from the British Library

Library of Congress Cataloging in Publication Data
Mason, Robin.
Elearning : the key concepts / Robin Mason and Frank Rennie.
p. cm.
Includes index.
ISBN 0–415–37306–9 (hardback : alk. paper) – ISBN 0–415–37307–7 (pbk. : alk.
paper) 1. Internet in education. 2. Computer-assisted instruction. 3. World Wide
Web. I. Rennie, Frank. II. Title.
LB1044.87.M27 2006
371.33′4678 – dc22 2005036125

ISBN10: 0–415–37306–9 (hbk)
ISBN10: 0–415–37307–7 (pbk)
ISBN10: 0–203–09948–6 (ebk)

ISBN13: 978–0–415–37306–7 (hbk)
ISBN13: 978–0–415–37307–4 (pbk)
ISBN13: 978–0–203–09948–3 (ebk)

CONTENTS

LIST OF KEY CONCEPTS

Accessibility
Active learning
Activity-based learning
Agent
Animations
Assessment
Asynchronous learning
Attachment
Audio/Video clips
Audioconference
Authentication
Avatar
Bandwidth
Bit/Byte
Blackboard
Blended learning
Blogging (Weblogging)
Bluetooth
Brainstorming
Broadband
Browser
Bulletin Board System (BBS)
Case study
Chatroom/Chatbox
Client
CMA
CMC
Collaborative Work/Learning
Communities
Computer Based Training (CBT)
Computer conferencing
Constructivism

Convergence
Cookie
Copyright
Corporate university
Course design
Courseware
CSCW
Cyberlearning
Cyberspace
Database
Desktop
Digital divide
Digitizing
Discussion board
Distributed education
Domain name
Download
Dropbox
Dual mode institutions
ECDL
Edutainment
Electronic forum
Email
Emoticons
Eportfolio
Experiential learning
Face-to-face (f2f)
Facilitator
FAQs
Feedback
File Transfer Protocol (FTP)
Firewall
Flaming (or flame war)
Flexible learning
Games and gaming
GIF
Global education
Graphics
Groupwork
Hacker
Hardware
Helpline/helpdesk

Hoax email
Homepage
HTML
HTTP
Hyperlink/Hypertext
Icon
ICQ
ICT
Information literacy
Instant messaging
Instructional design
Interaction
Internet
Internet café
Internet Service Provider (ISP)
Intranet
Java
JPEG
Killer app
LAN
Learning centre
Learning Management System (LMS)
Learning objects
Learning object repositories
Lifelong learning
Logon/off or Login/out
Lurking
Mental models
Mentoring
Meta tag
Metadata
MLE
Modem
Moderator
Module
MOO/MUD
Motivation
Multimedia
Multiple Choice Question (MCQ)
Netiquette
Netmeeting
Networks

Online
Online libraries
Open learning
Open source
Password
PDF
Peer-to-peer
Peer assessment
Plagiarism
Platform
Portal
Post or posting
Problem-based learning (PBL)
Quality assurance
Retention
Role play
Screen dump
Search engine
Self-directed learning
Semantic web
Server
Simulation
Situated learning
Skype
Snail mail
Social capital
Software
Spam
Student-centred learning – or Learner-centred learning
Surfing
Synchronous learning
Text messaging
Threaded discussion
TMA
Toolbar
Trojan
Trust
Tutor group
Tutoring
Upload
URL
Validation

Videoconferencing
Virtual reality
Virtual seminar
Virtual university
Virus
VLE
Voice-over-internet protocol (VoIP)
Web
Web-based learning
Web enabled
Web presence
Webcam
Webcast
WebCT
Webinar
Weblog
Webpage
WebQuests
Welcome page
Wiki
Wireless network
Worm

LIST OF FIGURES

NOTE

Throughout the book, references to key concept entries are shown in bold.

INTRODUCTION

Growth of elearning

Elearning, like other new technologies, has been the subject of wildly inaccurate predictions. The most commonly quoted is:

> The next big killer application for the Internet is going to be education. Education over the Internet is going to be so big it is going to make email usage look like a rounding error. (Chambers, 1999)

In fact, elearning has enjoyed a modest growth rate in both education and training, but nowhere near the growth that was first predicted. Nevertheless, an American study for 2004 found that **online** enrolments grew at rates faster than the overall student body, and universities expected the rates of growth to further increase (Allen and Seaman, 2004). A UK study has called the growth in elearning 'rapid', as institutions race to compete for a share of the increased and changing demand for higher education (O'Neill, Singh and O'Donoghue, 2004).

The growth in elearning has been fuelled by the growth in importance of **lifelong learning**. Relevant features of this movement are:

- the need to update knowledge and skills;
- the need to retrain, as jobs-for-life have all but vanished; and
- the need to maintain currency in the face of exploding information on the internet.

Related to this trend, Jung (2000) notes that in South Korea the lifelong learning laws were revised by the government to allow private educational institutions to grant degrees.

Definitions

What exactly is meant by the term elearning? In fact, the meaning has changed over time and has different nuances, for example, in education and in training, and in compulsory rather than in higher education.

Jay Cross is credited with coining the term elearning in 1998. He says:

> We thought we could take the instructors out of the learning process and let workers gobble up self-paced (i.e., 'don't expect help from us') lessons on their own. We were wrong. First-generation eLearning was a flop. (Jay Cross, n.d.)

Definitions of elearning abound on the **web** and each has a different emphasis: some focus on the content, some on the communication, some on the technology. One of the early definitions for elearning is ASTD's (American Society for Training & Development), who define it as covering a wide set of applications and processes, such as **web-based learning**, computer-based learning, virtual classrooms and digital collaboration. ASTD even includes the delivery of content via audio- and videotape, satellite broadcast, interactive TV and CD-ROM.[1]

Other definitions confine elearning to the use of the **internet**; for example:

> e-Learning refers to the use of internet technologies to deliver a broad array of solutions that enhance knowledge and performance. It is based upon three fundamental criteria:
>
> 1. It is networked.
> 2. It is delivered to the end–user via a computer using standard internet technology.
> 3. It focuses on the broadest view of learning. (Rosenberg, 2001)

Many definitions highlight the 'location' of the learning: e.g. the use of **network** technologies to create, foster, deliver and facilitate learning, anytime and anywhere.[2]

A simple yet comprehensive definition has been produced by the Open and Distance Learning Quality Council of the UK. It recognises the distinction between the content of learning and the process:

> E-Learning is the effective learning process created by combining digitally delivered content with (learning) support and services.[3]

Student satisfaction

The growth in elearning needs to be fuelled by students' acceptance and enthusiasm for the medium and their persistence in studying to the end of an online course, otherwise it will be short lived. Recent studies of student satisfaction with online learning are usually positive. For instance, a US study of college students' internet use (Jones and Madden, 2002) showed that 79 per cent agreed that internet use had had a positive impact on their academic experience. Nearly half believed that online communication enabled them to express ideas to a teacher that they would not have expressed in class.

There is conflicting evidence regarding student drop-out on online courses. Print-based distance education has traditionally had a lower persistence rate (**retention**) than campus-based education, but many studies of online education compare drop-out rates with campus education, not with distance education. Totally online learning bears more resemblance to distance education than it does to campus education, although there appears to be little direct comparison of these in academic publications: the learner is more isolated and therefore needs greater **motivation**; social contact is much reduced and is mediated by technology; finally, the skill of the instructor or **tutor** plays a significant role in the student experience.

An Australian study compared students' attitudes to online courses at two universities and found that factors such as content, personalised **feedback**, interface and learning **communities** were significantly related to students' satisfaction with **asynchronous** elearning systems. Well structured, high **quality** content that is presented in an easy to understand format, along with personalised feedback on their progress, are important elements of effective elearning. Coupled with these factors is the need to learn in a community, and the ability to select resources from the asynchronous elearning system to suit personal needs (Hisham, Campton and FitzGerald, 2004).

Terminology

There is a confusion of terms associated with elearning, partly because different English speaking countries have evolved slightly different uses, and partly because the English language is itself evolving as its use becomes increasingly widespread. The term elearning is relatively new and many words are used to describe roughly the same activity. For example, '**computer conferencing**' referred to the communications aspect of elearning before the advent of the web, then 'telelearning' had a brief ascendancy during the 1990s, but has fallen out of use now. The term **'web-based learning'** is still sometimes used, as are 'online learning', 'virtual classroom' and 'asynchronous learning'. On the whole, these words refer to the same practice; however, other terms are used by different writers as if they referred to the same practice, but in fact do not. One example is **'virtual university'** which can be an off-shoot of a university with a range of programmes taught entirely online, but can also refer to something that is neither a university nor 'virtually' online. Another such term is 'distance education' which in the UK usually implies print-based learning materials plus some form of **face-to-face** (**f2f**) or online **tutoring**, but which can refer to correspondence education, **videoconferencing** or even elearning in other parts of the world. Whatever the technology, distance education is a method rather than a philosophy of education. **'Open learning'**, on the other hand, is commonly used synonymously with distance education, but usually refers to the aim of removing barriers to learning e.g. for students with disabilities or with few prior qualifications. As such, it is a goal or an educational policy, which could apply to face-to-face as well as to online education (Bates, 2005). The term **'distributed education'** is an even more confusing term. Some writers use it synonymously with distance education; others imply something closer to **blended learning** and occasionally it seems to mean elearning.

One explanation for these differences lies in the way in which the user conceptualises the field i.e. which term is the overarching one containing other practices as a subset. For example, the term **'flexible learning'** is a favourite in Australia and in the following description refers to elearning as a subset of flexible learning.

> E-learning as a component of flexible learning describes a wide set of applications and processes which use any available electronic media in the pursuit of vocational education and training. It includes computer-based learning, web-based learning, virtual classrooms and digital collaboration. [Source: Australian Flexible Learning Framework for the National Vocational Education and Training System 2005–7]

Learning Circuits, an American glossary, makes elearning a subset of distance education: 'The definition of distance education is broader than and entails the definition of e-learning'.[4]

Our own hierarchy of terms is illustrated in Figure 1 and positions elearning as a type of distance education. Distributed education is a

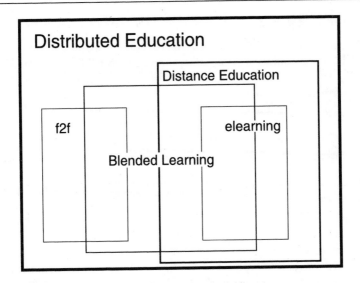

Figure 1 The relationship of elearning to distributed learning

broader term which includes aspects of distance and online education, as well as blending with face-to-face learning.

Although elearning seems to be used almost ubiquitously and has displaced many of the earlier words, the term '**blended learning**' still has synonyms e.g. 'adjunct mode' and 'hybrid teaching' which are both common in the US. In fact, any media-related term which is popularised undergoes the following trajectory: at first it is a buzz word; then it becomes over-used so the early-adopters move on to coin new words and concepts, and finally it either dies out completely or finds its rightful place as signifying a particular idea or practice. Already the early adopters of elearning are looking around for new words, or are adapting the term to cover new meanings. M-learning, meaning mobile elearning on the road or anywhere outside the office or home, is one of the new buzz words. Meanwhile, elearning is being redefined as 'enhanced' learning or even '**experiential**' **learning**.

These substitutions for 'electronic' reflect a realisation that it is not the electronic nature of elearning which captures its true value, but rather the opportunity to integrate working, learning and community in the workplace or university. Furthermore, the early elearning adopters have come full circle in rejecting an 'either-or' view of learning online versus learning face-to-face. This is why blended learning has become so popular.

Underlying theory

As elearning is the focus of much experimentation across a wide variety of disciplines and levels, it is perhaps too early to talk about an underlying theory to which the majority of researchers would subscribe. Nevertheless, **constructivism** does seem to be the approach most commonly evident in elearning courses. Bangert supports this view:

> The majority of the web-based courses today are designed using constructivist educational principles. (Bangert, 2004)

In the constructivist theory the emphasis is placed on the learner or the student rather than the teacher or the instructor. It is the learner who interacts with content and events, and thereby gains an understanding of the ideas or events. The learner, therefore, constructs his/her own conceptualisations and solutions to problems. Learner autonomy and initiative are not only accepted but actively encouraged. Furthermore, the process of discussion, reading other learners' messages and receiving feedback on one's own messages, provides the environment and scaffolding necessary for higher-order thinking (Slavin, 1994). Constructivist theory claims that this kind of thinking depends to some extent on a socio-cultural and communicative experience (Stacey, 1998).

The aim of constructivist principles as applied to elearning is to engender independent, self-reliant learners who have the confidence and skill to use a range of strategies to construct their own knowledge. Eklund *et al.* writing for the Australian Flexible Learning Framework, note:

> The attainment of higher-order knowledge, attitudes and approaches embedded in a social context and made all the more possible through technology is an aim of education in the post-modern society. (Eklund, Kay and Lynch, 2003)

Constructivist-based models frequently used in the online environment include:

- **situated learning**;
- **problem–based learning**;
- **communities** of practice;
- **simulations**.

The concept of situated learning has been developed by Lave and Wenger (1990):

Lave argues that learning as it normally occurs is a function of the activity, context and culture in which it occurs (i.e. it is situated). This contrasts with traditional classroom learning activities which involve knowledge which is often presented in an abstract form and out of context. Social **interaction** is a critical component of situated learning – learners become involved in a 'community of practice' which embodies certain beliefs and behaviors to be acquired. As the beginner or newcomer moves from the periphery of this community to its centre, they become more active and engaged within the culture and hence assume the role of expert or 'oldtimer'.[5]

Problem-based learning works very well with a constructivist approach as shown in the following definition by Barbara Duch:

> Problem-based learning (PBL) is an instructional method that challenges students to 'learn to learn,' working cooperatively in groups to seek solutions to real world problems. These problems are used to engage students' curiosity and initiate learning the subject matter. PBL prepares students to think critically and analytically, and to find and use appropriate learning resources.[6]

Online communities of practice provide an environment for learners to develop knowledge through interaction with others, in an environment where knowledge is created, nurtured and sustained. Because learning together is integral to community building, an important component of these online communities is that members develop a sense of belonging and mutual commitment. The training world has shown considerable interest in these online communities, as the Knowledge Management (KM) drive has begun to wane:

> Recently there has been a trend towards recognising that there are aspects of knowledge – broadly 'what people know' – which cannot be articulated, abstracted, codified, captured and stored. This is sometimes called 'less structured knowledge' in order to differentiate it from the codified 'structured knowledge' that was the focus of earlier KM approaches. (Hildreth and Kimble, 2002)

Simulations are particularly useful in demonstrating concepts in the hard sciences. In some cases, they provide interactive **multimedia** presentations which explain difficult or abstract concepts. In other cases, they are designed to model real scenarios and hence allow the learner to participate and experience without risk.

Related to the theory of constructivism is the notion of **self-directed learning**, defined as: a learning environment in which students are given a great deal of responsibility for and input into their own learning. The role of the teacher changes to a **facilitator** or guide. Associated terms or concepts include: andragogy, facilitated learning, learner-centredness. Instead of seeing self-directed learners as autonomous, isolated and individualistic, recent research has reinterpreted self-direction in a constructivist light. For instance, Merriam and Caffarella (1999) stress the social context of learning and the social construction of knowledge.

While many researchers would object to the idea that elearning is founded on a particular learning theory, perhaps it is possible to conclude that there are a cluster of related concepts around upon which most elearning courses are based.

Course design

The design of online courses is undoubtedly one of the critical components of successful elearning. How different is **course design** for elearning? One answer might be: not a lot. The caveat however, is that many elements of good course design are noticeably absent in campus-based lecture courses! Ewell (1997) refers to colleges and universities as 'novice cultures' in implementing even the most obvious aspects of what is known about good teaching and learning.

A review of one hundred research papers about elearning in higher education identified four major features of good practice (Coomey and Stephenson, 2001):

- *Dialogue*: using email, **bulletin boards**, 'real-time' chat, **asynchronous** chat, group discussions and debate, the tutor or **moderator** structures interactive opportunities into the content of the course;
- *Involvement*: includes responses in structured tasks, active engagement with material, collaboration and small group activities;
- *Support*: includes periodic **face-to-face** (**f2f**) contact, online tutorial supervision, **peer** support, advice from experts, feedback on performance, support services and **software** tools. Support is the most important feature of successful online courses, as reported in nearly all of the one hundred papers surveyed;
- *Control*: refers to the extent to which learners have control of key learning activities and are encouraged to exercise that control.

Encouraging dialogue in online courses is partly a question of good moderator skills: setting the right tone, starting with an appropriate ice-breaker activity, logging on regularly and responding to queries, comments or discussion points, and providing a range of media for dialogue (**synchronous** and asynchronous, **blogging** and **Wikis**, email and conferencing). However, some students are highly resistant to this form of learning; in fact, they do not see it as learning. Others perceive dialogue purely for chat and work against more serious discussion and exchange. Building discussion into the course **assessment** (by awarding marks for the quality of online contributions) may help, and close monitoring and commenting on messages by the tutor in the first weeks of the course may help to establish the appropriate tone.

Devising small group activities which can be carried out online is an important aspect of involving students in the course content. Some online course designers build peer commenting and **peer assessment** into their **collaborative** activities (McConnell, 2002; Collis *et al.*, 2002). Others use online debates (Mason, 2000), group assignments and structured activities (Salmon, 2002). Individual activities might involve finding particular online resources, making a presentation to the group, contributing to a **database** or writing an analysis of a paper or website for access by the group. The aim of all these activities, whether collaborative or individual, is to involve the learner in the course content, and in learning through engagement with ideas and other learners.

Supporting students in the learning process is, not surprisingly, the feature they most value. On the academic side, individual feedback on assigned work and providing comments and summaries in online discussions are two support methods appropriate to elearning. On the networking side, systems need to be in place for helping students with technical queries i.e. offline, a telephone **helpdesk**, and online, a conference for questions, and a series of **FAQs** for common problems. On the administrative side, processes for handling registration, payment and withdrawal should be easy and transparent. A course handbook, assignment guide and calendar should all be available online, as well as a facility for communicating course news and updates.

While students want good support from their tutor and their educational organisation, they also want more control of their learning experience than is usual in a campus-based course. Elearning should provide flexibility in the time and location of access, so online activities, collaborative group work and debates and discussions should have more time allocated to them than would be necessary if students were co-located. Designing courses with a choice of content is also possible and helps learners develop self-direction and can attract a wider range of students (Mason *et al.*, 2005).

As learners become increasingly sophisticated media users, they will expect more of their elearning than simple text. Multimedia, **graphics, animations**, music and **audio/video clips** are all relatively easy to build into course materials and in some curriculum areas, are necessary to convey the content adequately. In addition, it is important to consider various kinds of motivational components: game elements, novelty and surprise features, humour and adventure activities, although any of these may not stand up to comparison with commercial products.

One of the big advantages of elearning course design is the ease with which it is possible to use a wide range of learning resources. The web provides almost unlimited access to materials which can enrich and support content developed specifically for the course. Electronic journals, many with free, open access to full text papers, are increasingly available. It is also possible to develop a 'webliography' with copyright clearance for papers used on a particular course or programme. Leaving students to find appropriate resources by browsing the web themselves is not usually advisable especially for undergraduates, as they can waste valuable study time. Nevertheless, with support and advice from the tutor, the use of web resources can provide an excellent focus for individual and group activities, as well as for the development of self-directed learning.

Good course design is more critical in the virtual environment than in face-to-face teaching, and it is more difficult to hide poor design or mediocre content. Many of the principles of elearning design are closer to those of print-based distance education and require institutional level processes; for example,

- **Assessment** needs to be fit for purpose, as does the blend of online and face-to-face elements;
- **Quality assurance** procedures for checking web content has internal consistency, and for maintaining the links to external web-sites, need to be put in place;
- Workload for both students and tutors needs to be carefully gauged at the outset and monitored regularly throughout the life of the course – it is very easy to overload students and this leads to superficial learning; it is also easy to overload tutors by expecting too much online interaction from them;
- Monitoring procedures for tutors should be in place so that students receive consistent support and fair marking of their assignments;

complaints from students must be followed up and systems devised for handling poor performance;

- Web content should be assessed for performance against the aims and objectives set by the course designers. Can the learner reasonably be expected to achieve what is stated with the materials provided?
- Navigation through the website should allow students to find their own way through the material, possibly by providing a course map.

Online course design must involve the provision of feedback to the learner, ideally through interaction with the tutor, the content and other learners. Feedback has been identified as 'probably the most powerful process that teachers and other learners can regularly use to affect a learner's performance' (Wlodkowski, 1999: 244). Comments on assignments by the tutor should never be negative and should indicate how the student could improve future performance. Comments on messages in an online discussion are another form of feedback, and come from other students as well as from the tutor. They need to be timely and take the discussion forward. Messages which simply acknowledge a student's submission add 'noise' to the system, not feedback. The design of the interface is another form of feedback (Simm, 2003), as the learner needs to establish a **mental model** of the environment in order to navigate around the system and achieve the learning goals.

Online assessment

Networked technologies are changing the nature of higher education, both for campus and distance learners, not only in the methods of delivery, but also in the content and skills being taught. However, on the whole, assessment strategies have not kept pace with the changes – both positive and negative – that online learning is precipitating. In order for the benefits of these changes to be fully realised in improved learning outcomes, it is essential that assessment be rethought for the new environment that communication technology has helped to create.

While many educators are convinced of the potential benefits of the online environment, it would be unwise to ignore the new problems created by the ease of access to vast amounts of electronic data. In relation to assessment, one of these problems is **plagiarism** which has taken on new forms and is undermining traditional coping strategies. Another issue arises with the spread of **global education** which communication technology encourages: 'how do you know that the student who carries out an online assignment is the student whom you eventually accredit?'

It is not a coincidence that the dominant pedagogy (in the West at least), centres on the value of interactivity, of collaborative learning, and of active engagement with the learning material. All these values are strongly supported in the online environment by the multimedia and communication potential of the web. However, most traditional forms of assessment (individual essays, **multiple choice questions** and invigilated exams) are not very appropriate for testing the skills and learning outcomes which elearning courses are promoting. Consequently students are reporting a mismatch between the values of the course pedagogy and the demands of the assessment.

The web has spawned a whole new generation of multiple choice testing software which offers benefits to academics teaching larger and larger classes in the form of relief from the burden of marking and benefits to students in terms of greater opportunity for feedback. At the other end of the assessment spectrum, the resource and communications potential of the web has facilitated a whole range of collaborative, interactive and **student-centred** forms of assessment which offer real learning opportunities for students.

It has been argued (Boud, 2000) that traditional assessment fails to provide opportunities for students to learn the very thing they most need to know: how to assess their own learning. One of the aims of higher education must surely be to prepare students for an increasingly unknowable future. Undergraduates and lifelong learners alike are increasingly realising that they must take responsibility for remaining employable. There is a need for programmes in which students reach not just immediate course-related goals but much wider learning and self-development goals.

Existing assessment practices frequently disempower learners and put the control and the judgement of learning in the hands of the assessors and tutors. In a learning society, it is the individual student who needs to develop the skills to assess their own and others' materials, to make judgements about quality and value, to give and receive feedback. One of the most significant tasks of the tutor is to help students develop these lifelong learning skills. Elearning is an ideal vehicle for providing just this opportunity. It is flexible so that those in employment can fit updating courses around their job; it is particularly successful with adult learners who are self-motivated and strategic learners; it adapts well to a peer-commenting, collaborative learning context.

However, the trap in all assessment activities is to fragment and compartmentalise knowledge and understanding for the sake of having a manageable process which fits the time and process constraints of common assessment methods. As a result, many existing assessment practices have effects which actually contradict lifelong learning outcomes. If developing lifelong learners is a core objective of higher education, the assessment processes need to be re-thought and re-positioned at the heart of the learning environment.

Examples of good practice in elearning approaches to assessment include the following:

- Feedback loops in which students have the opportunity to apply the results of tutor feedback on their assignments to show improved performance;
- Group assignments in which students have opportunities to develop team working skills;
- Opportunities for students to engage in the construction and reconstruction of criteria for judging work;
- Practice in discernment to identify critical aspects of problems and issues;
- Opportunities to comment on other students' work as well as to assess their own work.

There are a number of hurdles to overcome in re-positioning assessment at the forefront of the course design process. One of these is the conservative attitude (and current workload) of instructors. The other is institutional policies, standards and practicalities in managing and resourcing assessment processes.

Researchers of elearning have often concluded that there is a need for a culture change amongst academics, course designers and students – to value self-examination, reflection and continuous improvement. It is commonly acknowledged that most academics receive little reward or compensation for devoting extra time to the design and development of online courses. Likewise, strategic learners will often avoid a course which has a reputation for being hard work. These factors make the re-thinking of assessment a challenging undertaking.

Assessment practices on virtual courses are on the whole much more innovative than in **face-to-face (f2f)** teaching. Multiple choice assignments have become more sophisticated, challenging and media-rich on the web, although they are obviously more demanding and time consuming to produce. In addition, online assignments can be collaborative, peer-marked, or presented electronically to the other students; they can be based around online activities, debates or discussion, and they can be marked and then made accessible for other students to read. In short, **ICT** supports assessment which is more demanding, more representative of the skills which the course is developing and more integrated with course content. McConnell's research confirms this:

> Collaborative review and assessment help students move away from dependence on lecturers as the only or major source of judgement about the quality of learning to a more autonomous and independent situation where each individual develops the experience, know-how and skill to assess their own learning. It is likely that this skill can be transferred to other lifelong learning situations and contexts. Equipping learners with such skills should be a key aspect of the so-called 'learning society'.
> (McConnell, 2002: 89)

Role of the tutor

Online teachers have a key role in creating a vibrant learning environment and in fostering a strong sense of community both through their teaching style and their attitude to the students. In this sense, teaching online is no different from teaching face-to-face. Good teachers care about their students' learning.

Nevertheless, for most academics, designing a course for the web is quite a change from preparing a series of lectures. Apart from the need to re-think the content, the student activities and the support mechanism, there is the unusual, for many, experience of having to work in a team. What was once a very private performance to a group of students, becomes a team effort often involving critical commenting on drafts of the print or web materials.

This form of 'public exposure' is only the beginning of the change from lecturing. Even for academics who already work in distance education, a much more significant change is required to tutor online courses in which students dominate the interactions and the tutor becomes a guide and facilitator. This constructivist, collaborative model of learning is hardly a new phenomenon, but it has become the dominant paradigm in most online courses. Across many areas of the curriculum, there is a greater emphasis on learning how to find out, rather than on learning what the teacher knows. This change can be unsettling for the teacher and also requires a new attitude to learning on the part of the student.

Nevertheless, there are many benefits. The pioneers of the new online learning courses report renewed interest and even excitement in the rewards of working closely with students, in nurturing an environment for learning, in guiding students through the maze of online resources by good course design and interaction in online discussions. Some have found a new career, often towards the end of a traditional one, reworking their tried and true teaching strategies for the new medium of the web or in some cases, multimedia CD-ROMs. In fact, there is evidence that one of the main elements in the success of many technology-based courses is the very renewed attention given to the teaching and learning processes which these technologies have demanded of academics. Instead of repeating the same content in lectures year in and year out, the academic can distil the ideas into course content either through print, the web, or multimedia. Then the focus can be on the more dynamic and interactive side of learning. For example, one academic comments:

> I contend that this possibility presents faculty with an exciting and stimulating opportunity to rethink, and to reinvent, their functions and responsibilities and their relationships to students. (Jackson, 2004)

Many studies, however, report that on the whole, faculties need more IT support than their institutions provide, and that students enter higher education with greater information technology abilities than their lecturers (Stephens and Creaser, 2002; Eklund, Kay and Lynch, 2003). Both of these barriers can deter a faculty from engaging with elearning.

The early adopters of online teaching have been very innovative pedagogically, for example, by experimenting with various kinds of assessment, by adapting collaborative activities to the online environment and by developing activities and resources to support online content. On the whole, however, the pedagogy of elearning has not kept pace with developments in the technology and the uptake of networked communication amongst young learners. The explanation given for this deficit is usually that academics are more interested in research than teaching and with the increasing pressures on universities to 'do more with less', academics simply do not have the time to devote to reflecting on how to teach their subject in a more facilitative manner. Rovai and Jordan note that faculty tend to teach the way they were taught:

> Since faculty promotion and tenure, at present, are largely based on research and publication, some professors zealously feel that they should not take away from their research or writing time to change curricula and pedagogy, for the potential rewards are not worth the time or risk to them. Consequently, many professors still use the traditional lecture as their instructional strategy of choice. (Rovai and Jordan, 2004)

There is conflicting evidence about the time demands of online teaching. A few studies in which teachers have been required to keep logs of all their work for online courses compared to **face-to-face (f2f)** teachers, have shown that the time demands for online teaching are different, but not more extensive (Thompson, 2004). However, questionnaire surveys of online faculty tend to be more 'impressionistic' and usually report that the majority of teachers think online courses are more time consuming than campus courses (Jones and Johnson-Yale, 2005).

The need for teachers to develop the skills to be a good online tutor has led to the growth of (usually online) courses. These provide tips and techniques for managing online discussions, but more importantly, they give participants the experience of being in an online environment and contributing messages to a group discussion. This is the best way of understanding what developing an online community is all about.

The role of the elearning tutor should be to provide the student with the opportunity to elearn, that is, to learn using the facilities and affordances of the online environment. The need to learn facts and information has vastly reduced and the ability to find, manipulate, analyse, synthesise and re-purpose information has increased concomitantly. One of the key resources in developing these abilities is other people. Gone are the threats that machines will replace teachers; machines can store, link and process information, but people transform it and add value to it. Tutors, mentors and online facilitators are now seen as the asset that makes all the difference to student retention, motivation and acceptance of elearning. Likewise, CBT (**computer-based training**) put up on the web with no human support, is increasingly seen as unsuccessful and a 'horseless-carriage' use of connectivity (Reynolds *et al.*, 2002). Because there is so much information available on the net, what is valued is knowing how to cope with it. Connecting with other people to share the load, to exchange tips and models for managing information, and to express ideas and give feedback, have become the essential elements of elearning methodology (Rennie and Mason, 2004).

Role of the student

For students, the primary reason for taking an elearning course is the flexibility it provides to study when and where they like. Students on graduate courses are frequently in full-time employment; undergraduate students are increasingly working part-time and need to fit their education around their job. At least one study shows that non-traditional students were satisfied with asynchronous interaction, whereas traditional learners preferred some synchronous interaction (Preston, 2004). The non-traditional learner i.e. a student who is not full-time, campus-based and just graduated from secondary school, now forms the majority in US higher education. Similarly in the UK, the heterogeneity of learners in the mass higher education system makes it difficult to meet the resultant variety of needs, because those who are direct entrants from school to full-time first degrees may well have different goals and competences to those who are mature, those who are time- or distance-challenged, or those who are taking higher degrees or continuing professional development courses.

Online learning can encourage reticent students, who might not flourish in a **face-to-face (f2f)** environment, to participate actively when those visual barriers are removed. Students working in their second language often find elearning beneficial because they can take as much time as they need to read material or messages and to write their responses.

While students are generally positive about elearning, there is undoubtedly resistance to the move to **student-centred**, self-directed learning, particularly amongst the traditional students. They are usually right in thinking it is more work, more time-consuming and more demanding intellectually than taking notes from a lecturer who tells them most of what they need to know for the final exam. Online learning skills – e.g. finding, using and discriminating amongst web-based materials – are also not ubiquitous, and lack of technical expertise – e.g. recovering from various forms of computer failures – is another negative feature of elearning. Some universities have recognised the need to support students in the transition to online and self-directed learning, by providing or developing web-based materials about online study skills and search techniques, and by scaffolding their courses so that students can adapt to the change in teaching approach.[7] Induction training courses are often run on campus for students to practice basic computer skills and to familiarise themselves with the online environment.

Surveys tend to show that students do not want elearning to replace face-to-face teaching entirely (e.g. Guri-Rosenblit, 2005); in short, some form of blended learning is the preferred option. A number of universities that introduced online courses as a way of attracting new learners, have found to their dismay that their campus students opt for these courses, often creating their own blend by taking one online course plus several face-to-face courses (Young, 2002).

Elearning creates new opportunities for many kinds of disabled learners:

- It is ideal for those who cannot travel to a campus;
- With enlarged fonts, it can be effective for the visually impaired;
- Using audio playback, it can work for the blind;
- For deaf students it generally works very well.

In fact, some practitioners claim that there is no disability that cannot be overcome with some form of adaptive technology.

The Special Educational Needs and Disability Act 2001 came into force in September 2002 in the UK, and makes it unlawful to discriminate against students with a disability. An accessible online resource should not mean one which in any way diminishes the learning experience or outcome. Students may have mobility difficulties, may be deaf or hard of hearing, be blind or have impaired vision. Some students may have learning difficulties, for example dyslexia. Others may have unseen disabilities, or a temporary injury or illness which requires additional support. Educational institutions are expected to make reasonable attempts to accommodate all of these limitations.

One example of how a piece of software can discriminate against the disabled involves the use of PowerPoint (PP). On blended learning courses, this is a popular tool, which is used extensively to support the delivery of face-to-face lectures. Increasingly, tutors are making their PowerPoint presentations available online. Screen readers cannot read the text on PP slides, which means that a visually impaired student will be unable to access a PP presentation. A 'reasonable adjustment' would be to make the content from PP presentation available as a **webpage** or as a document which could be displayed in a word processor and hence described by a screen reader.

Online community

More has been written about online community – whether it exists, how to foster it, what distinguishes it from face-to-face communication – than any other aspect of elearning.

A typical approach to the research of online community is that conducted by Rovai (2001). He identifies four essential elements of successful community development:

- The creation of a group identity (spirit);
- The exchange of honest feedback (**trust**);
- The quality of interaction amongst participants (interaction);
- The contribution to learning that the exchanges make (learning).

There is conflicting evidence as to whether this kind of online community can be developed totally online. An initial **face-to-face (f2f)** meeting certainly seems to help or at least speed up the process (Jarvenpaa et al., 1998). It is usual that not all of the students in a particular cohort join in the online community; the most vocal, confident or experienced online students tend to dominate the discussions and report in feedback forms that they found the online community supportive and beneficial to their learning.

Failure to develop an online community is not uncommon in online courses: if students have no real reason to **log on**, if messages and queries go unanswered, if technical difficulties prevent access, or if the online environment is unstructured, students soon conclude that their study time is better spent on other aspects of learning. There is no doubt, however, that some students and teachers do experience online groups in which members are valued, their inputs contribute to the learning environment and participants enjoy logging on. This sense of community has very positive effects on the learning outcomes of the course (Brown, 2001).

Successful online discussions are significantly different from the kinds of face-to-face discussions that take place in the traditional classroom. First, all students have a voice and second, the asynchronous nature of the activity means that participants can reflect on what they write before **posting** it. Third, it is difficult for any one person, including the teacher, to control the flow or direction of the interaction. Fourth, contrary to expectations about the coldness of virtual communication, the online community is often 'hyperpersonal'.

> Participants in online discussion seem to project their personalities into it, creating feelings of presence that build online learning communities. (Swan, 2003: 148)

Many online courses 'require' students to participate in the discussions by awarding marks for the quality of each learner's messages. The pedagogical rationale is that it validates online discussion as a vehicle for learning. In addition, it helps to create community and reduce social isolation. Mayes argues that:

> It is likely that greater insight into pedagogic innovation is to be gained through focusing on the social dimensions of communities of learners than on continuing to view the learner's key relationships as being with the subject matter, or at best with a tutor. (Mayes, 2002)

He goes on to say that the way in which learners identify with particular communities will determine the most fundamental way they think and feel about learning, and as a result:

All learning is situated in a personal, social and organisational context, which determines motivation. (Mayes, 2002)

Blended learning

Blended or hybrid courses mix online and **face-to-face** (**f2f**) components. In fact, courses in which there is even a minor online component (e.g. a supporting website, **email** access to the instructor, an online reading list) are sometimes referred to as elearning courses. Furthermore, all courses blend a range of learning media or learning opportunities: at the most basic level, they involve thinking, reading and blending new information with existing knowledge.

The term blended learning was originally used to describe courses which tried to combine the best of face-to-face and online learning. As the term became popular, more and more combinations were referred to as blended learning: for example, combining a range of technologies, a range of teaching methods, a range of learning experiences, or a range of locations of the learning events. Though the term continues to be used, it is beginning to lose all meaning.

One example where the term leads to useful research results is a study which examines the relationship of a sense of community across three modes of learning: the traditional classroom, blended, and fully online higher education learning environments. The authors provide evidence which suggests that blended courses produce a stronger sense of community among students than either traditional or fully online courses (Rovai and Jordan, 2004). In a study of the workplace over two years, Barbian (2002) concludes that blended learning methods boost employee productivity over single-delivery options.

The blended solutions commonly used are: 50/50 models of face-to-face and online learning which combine the best of both worlds; even 75 per cent online with one face-to-face or residential meeting is successful in overcoming the limitations of online learning while benefiting from its overall cost-effectiveness and flexibility.

Importantly, blended approaches can encourage participants to make *better* use of face-to-face contact in the knowledge that preparations and follow up can be conducted online. Totally online courses should be reserved for those contexts in which it is impossible or unreasonable for learners to come together – typically international events and training courses, or projects in which learners cannot leave their operational setting. Synchronous technologies provide a partial substitute.

The learning platform

A range of software has been developed to support elearning: a virtual learning environment (**VLE**) and a managed learning environment (**MLE**) are the terms used in the UK, but course management system (CMS) and **learning management system (LMS)** are used in the US.

A VLE provides the facilities for presenting content, for online communication, for assessment and for tracking student activity. Many VLEs contain basic authoring tools to enable academics with limited web experience to place teaching resources online. An MLE refers to the whole range of information systems and processes which educational institutions use to manage learning. An MLE, therefore, includes the VLE, and in addition, the systems for registration and student records, for finances and other business processes, and also all of the aspects of quality control.

Proprietary VLE software generally provides the features listed in Figure 2. VLEs are used to support **face-to-face (f2f)** teaching and blended courses as well as fully online elearning. As a support for campus courses, the VLE is used to distribute lecture notes, overheads and other support materials, and to provide access to additional readings and websites. On blended courses, the VLE might be the means of communication amongst students and the tutor, and would be the vehicle for students to work with computer-based materials such as simulations, quizzes and interactive tutorials. Online self-assessment questions which provide feedback are an increasingly popular means for students to check their understanding of course materials, and are often provided on blended courses. With fully online courses, the VLE facilitates all aspects: the course content, supporting resources, online discussion, collaborative work and submission of assessment.

As proprietary VLEs increase in price and other systems develop more desirable features, the problem of switching to another VLE and having to transfer course materials from one environment to another, has caused some concern. This has led to a preference for **open source** software, which is usually free and customisable to suit the context of the particular educational organisation. Of course, while the software itself may be free, the maintenance and adaptation to the individual organisation are not, and generally require a support team in order that open source systems are a viable option.

Trends in elearning

Until recently, many discussions of elearning were about the technology

Features	Examples
Communication between tutors and students	E-mail, discussion boards and virtual chat facilities which support various types of communication: synchronous and asynchronous, one-to-one, one-to-many and many-to-many.
Self-assessment and summative assessment	Multiple-choice assessment with automated marking and immediate feedback.
Delivery of learning resources and materials	Through the provision of learning and teaching materials, images and video clips, links to other web resources, online discussion and assessment activities.
Shared work group areas	Allows designated groups of students to upload and share files as well as communicate with each other.
Support for students	Could take the form of communication with tutors or other students, provision of supporting materials such as course information and Frequently Asked Questions (FAQs).
Student tools	Individual student web pages, 'drop boxes' for the upload of coursework, electronic diaries and calendars.
Management and tracking of students	Usernames and passwords to ensure that only registered students can access the course; analysis of assessment undertaken by students or their use of materials within the VLE.
Consistent and customisable look and feel	A standard user interface that is easy for students to understand and use. Courses can be individualised with colours, graphics and logos – but the essential mode of use remains constant.
Navigation structure	Structured delivery of information supported by a standard navigation toolbar. Most VLE software assumes that students will work their way through linear sequences of instructional material. Others are more flexible and will accommodate alternative information structures, e.g. multi-path case studies.

Figure 2 Table from the Social Work and Social Policy Website[8]

aspects. For example, a very common opening gambit to explain elearning would focus on learning anything, 'anyplace', at 'anytime'. The discussion would highlight the flexibility of elearning and move into the technologies which support learners accessing a course outside the classroom context. While elearning is undoubtedly more flexible than **face-to-face** (**f2f**), campus-based learning, there have always been pedagogical and social limits to totally flexible learning. Asynchronous discussions on a course may last for several weeks, but they do not last indefinitely; studies of logon times show that students do input messages over the full 24 hours, but evening time from 6pm until midnight accounts for by far the majority of usage. (Harasim, 1990)

There are three technologies which are just beginning to see a major uptake and hence might have a major impact on elearning:

Broadband

Cheap, unlimited **bandwidth** is not yet a reality, however, if and when it does arrive, it should give an extremely big boost to elearning. Real-time events for students at a distance would add a new dimension to elearning. For example, tutorials and small group meetings could be held over software such as **Netmeeting** or **Skype** which provide video, audio and shared **desktop** facilities. Groove messaging offers near-instant communication as well as confidentiality and shared files, and other software provides buddy systems that allow students to be in close contact with their peers. Activities could be based around these facilities whereby students engage in peer commenting, team projects and self-help groups. **Webcasting** using guest lectures, offers immediacy and the opportunity to engage in discussion with experts and special advisers. The fact that the lecture can be stored and accessed after the event provides flexibility as well as immediacy.

Most of these real-time activities are difficult, costly or actually impossible over dial-up lines. **Broadband** offers course designers the opportunity to design courses using the optimal mix of synchronous and asynchronous modalities, without concern about disadvantaging remote users.

Mobile technologies

The 'anyplace' aspect used to promote elearning is becoming somewhat more realistic with the advent of **wireless**, mobile learning (mlearning) e.g. from a mobile telephone, wireless laptop, PDA or tablet PC. Personal Digital Assistants (PDAs), also known as palmtops and handheld PCs, fit into the hand and are generally very portable, capable of being carried in a jacket pocket, for example. They were first developed as electronic organisers, or personal information managers. These contain information such as diaries, address books and task lists. They eventually evolved into mini PCs, able to carry out limited PC tasks such as word and spreadsheet processing, and nowadays most are capable of web browsing and email functions via cables connected to **networks**. PDAs also offer infrared communication, allowing data to be transferred across short distances between units without the need for networks. Many PDAs come with docking stations in order for them to be connected to desktop computers, allowing data to be synchronised between the two devices. The tablet PC is an adaptation of the laptop. It is available in two styles: either with a keyboard (known as a 'convertible' tablet) or without a keyboard (known as a 'slate' tablet, and generally slimmer and more lightweight than the convertible). Convertible tablets normally have detachable or foldable keyboards, and all tablet PCs have touch-sensitive screens, usually A4 in size, which require stylus pens for input. They are generally much quicker to boot up than desktop PCs. The tablet can be used either in portrait or landscape mode, and uses wireless technology for connection to the internet or other networks (Wood, 2003).

For the moment, these technologies are used not for accessing the content of courses, but for communication, administration and other peripheral aspects of studying e.g. ordering books from the library. One area of potential use is for taking photos or notes when on field trips. Another advantage is the stylus pen used with tablet PCs which is more convenient for web browsing than a mouse. However, these devices currently have limited storage capacity and their batteries require regular charging or data can be lost.

Wireless and WiFi networking need to become more popular before mlearning will boost the feasibility of learning anyplace and anytime. The trend, however, is for these devices to converge, so that mobile phones will adopt PDA functions and tablets will adopt more of the functionality of desktop PCs.

Podcasting

Podcasting is a form of broadcasting over the internet. With podcasting, learners can **download** lectures and pictures to their PC or portable digital device to access at their convenience. This is a very different learning scenario from reading text on a computer screen, or from sitting in a lecture hall. Using an iPod or similar device, the learner listens to the content, which could talk them through diagrams, **graphics**, photos or paintings, or could be a discussion between two experts with opposing views. Language learning, music studies and other subjects with a strong oral component have obvious applications. This approach to learning will appeal to learners who prefer to take in information aurally rather than through text and circumvents the problems of a mini screen, which limits the use of mobile phones for learning. Podcasts can provide students with a means of reviewing material, especially non-native speakers. Podcasts can be used more informally by teachers to provide feedback on group assignments or presentations, or to provide supplementary material for a blended course.

Duke University experimented with providing 1,600 first year students with an iPod, in 2004. The evaluation report notes five broad areas of use:

- course content dissemination;
- classroom recording;
- field recording;
- study support;
- file storage and transfer (Belanger, 2005).

The supporting technologies of podcasting are relatively inexpensive and easy to use. Like blogging, students can be producers of content, rather than passive receivers. The portable and on-demand nature of podcasting makes it a technology with potential for elearning (Meng, 2005).

Conclusion

The Internet has been called a disruptive technology, that is, one that significantly changes the way people and systems operate. Teaching online is not a process that can be controlled in the way that **face-to-face (f2f)** lecturing can be. In the online environment, the teacher becomes a facilitator, guide or even expert resource, but no longer the sole determiner of the student experience. The internet is too vast; the impact of student-to-student communication too great; the asynchronicity of the environment too ephemeral to control. The learner now decides when and where to log on, how to work through the course materials, what resources to draw upon, who to work with collaboratively, when to contribute to discussions, and so on. While this self-directedness is hugely welcomed by many students – and particularly those who are confident, self-motivated and resourceful learners – it is not universally successful with all learners. Those who have poor study habits, lack self-discipline or motivation, have been educationally disadvantaged, or are driven almost solely by extrinsic reasons for wanting a degree, tend to find the student-centred pedagogy bewildering, too demanding or too much hard work. In any case, students do need a gradual process of learning to be self-directed. They need training and practice in ICT skills of searching, analysing and managing web-based resources; they need a student-friendly online environment which encourages and rewards interaction, and they need supportive tutoring to help them adapt their study patterns from linear working through textbooks and lecture notes to interactive engagement with ideas, resources and other students.

Elearning is not the answer to all educational problems or suitable in all contexts. It is rather limited for teaching some practical or physical skills; it requires more up-front preparation time than lecturing; it does not provide the range of interaction, support and socialisation that face-to-face teaching can offer. Despite these shortcomings, elearning, whether as an adjunct to campus-based learning or as a totally online offering, is gaining in acceptance and growing in use.

Notes

1 http://www.learningcircuits.org/glossary.html
2 http://agelesslearner.com/intros/elearning.html
3 http://www.odlqc.org.uk/odlqc/n19-e.htm
4 http://www.learningcircuits.org/glossary.html
5 http://www.educationau.edu.au/archives/cp/04k.htm
6 http://www.udel.edu/pbl/
7 http://www.lc.unsw.edu.au/olib.html;   http://www.bangor.ac.uk/studyskills/skillsindex.htm; http://www.ucc.vt.edu/stdysk/stdyhlp.html
8 http://www.swap.ac.uk/elearning/using5.asp?version=textversion

KEY CONCEPTS

ACCESSIBILITY

In terms of elearning, accessibility generally has two specific meanings. Computer accessibility refers to the usability of a computer system by individual users. This would cover disabilities such as colour blindness, dyslexia, sound impairment and lack of manual dexterity. **Web** accessibility generally refers to the increasingly common practice of making pages on the **internet** accessible to all users, regardless of whether they access via a slow **modem** or a state-of-the-art **broadband** connection. An example might be that large files or complex **graphics** may be impossible to **download** without a high **bandwidth** connection, resulting in the 'freezing' of the system and frustration to the potential user. The key to a consideration of accessibility is to enable users to access information in their own preferred manner, and so this is closely related to the thoughtful design of **distributed education**. In making computers and the web accessible, careful planning can enhance usability for all users, not just those with specific disabilities. Examples are that some users may prefer text links rather than **icons**, while the incorporation of sound files to accompany images does not simply benefit users with a visual impairment. The ability for individual users to self-select the level of accessibility required, for example for a colour-blind user to select a particular colour scheme on the screen, is a feature that is increasingly being built into public-access internet sites.

Web links

Web accessibility initiative: http://www.w3.org/WAI
Web content accessibility guidelines: http://www.w3.org/TR/WAI-WEBCONTENT

ACTIVE LEARNING

Refers to techniques where students do more than simply listen to a lecture. The notion is not new and not a product of elearning. However, it has been given added impetus through elearning, which is strongly associated with many forms of active learning: **constructivism, self-directed learning, interaction** and those processes which engage the learner in an active rather than passive mode.

Adapting active learning to the **online** environment usually involves dialogue with the teacher or other learners, observing or taking part in

case studies, role plays or **simulations**. There is often resistance to active learning by students who are accustomed to lectures or students who prefer passive learning. It is important therefore to prepare students through explaining the objectives of active learning and offering support in the initial stages.

ACTIVITY-BASED LEARNING

This is not a precisely defined term and is usually thought of in opposition to passive learning. It marks a shift away from content-based learning which is associated with lectures and some forms of distance education. The underlying theory is that people learn by doing and that experience is the basis of all learning. Allied with the element of activity is the notion of reflection, and together these two form a cyclic process: action and reflection on action.

AGENT

A particular type of **software** application designed in such a way that it can take a variety of 'decisions' based upon the design constraints of its programmers. Agents have been used to create the appearance of a person with whom the user can have different levels of **interaction** and carry out a number of basic tasks or enquiries. At least one European university has used a sophisticated agent to create a **helpline** 'problem page' facility by introducing new students to the 'character' of their agent who can 'discuss' with other students a range of study problems and possible solutions. A measure of the success of this agent is that several students have apparently attempted to date her!

ANIMATIONS

Essentially these are moving drawings that can be used to illustrate sequential stages in a process (e.g. a flow diagram of a project) or give the impression of moving parts (e.g. a schematic diagram of how a car engine operates). Animations can be used in combination with text, sound and **hyperlinks** to create a rich **online** learning environment that improves on simple text and/or still photographs on a printed page. Complex or interlinked animations can be used to create a **network** of special effects that can be used to illustrate events online where **video**

clips are not possible or appropriate. An example of this is the illustration of the geological sequence of the movement of the continents into their present position available at http://pgap.uchicago.edu/PGAPhome. html. Animations are created by drawing a series of images of an object and making small changes to each image to simulate movement. The greater the number of individual images to a movement, then the smoother will be the apparent transition. Animations have been used on CD as a learning resource in **distributed education**, and as more users gain access to higher **bandwidth** over the **internet** (such as **broadband**) then it becomes easier to incorporate animations in **webpages** or the managed learning environment (**MLE**). An obstacle to their use over lower bandwidths is that the large number of images required for very detailed animations produces large, complex files that move very slowly (if at all) on slow data transmission lines. As an example, compare the moving image of Gondwanaland at http://kartoweb.itc.nl/gondwana/gondwana_gif.html. This is a large and complex file so will require a fast **web** access. Animations are ideal for online tuition in subjects such as geology and environmental sciences where it is impossible to film footage of past events, or for medicine or nuclear science where it would be dangerous and/or unethical to conduct 'live' experiments.

Illustrations of animated clipart at: http://www.animationfactory.com
*Virtual **courseware** in geology and environmental sciences can be found at:* http://www.sciencecourseware.com

ASSESSMENT

A general term for the process used to give a value to a learner's knowledge and/or progress in attaining relevant skills. We can broadly classify assessments into two types, *formative* through which learners can test their understanding of a subject before moving on to other stages, and *summative* assessments which will count towards the overall grade or mark obtained by a learner for a particular piece of work. Normally a formative assessment does not count towards a final grade, but rather it gives learners an indication of their progress and level of attainment to allow them to fully form their ideas. Formative assessments may be designated as self-assessment exercises that remain with the learner, or they can be required to submit the work to a **tutor** or perhaps to an **electronic forum** where it is open to scrutiny by the class. Good practice dictates that assessments should be related to predefined learning outcomes for a **module** or a particular piece of work. Increasingly it is common that assessments will also be linked to a pre-agreed marking strategy to enable an audit of the allocation of marks, and this may be shown to learners in advance of attempting the assessment in order to indicate areas of importance.

Due to some of the initial concerns relating to elearning, such as 'how do we know that the person being assessed is actually doing the assessment?' it is significant that the standards and controls on elearning assessment have pushed the barriers towards good practice for educational assessments in general. The difficulties of working remotely and with **asynchronous** access have forced tutors and teachers to be very clear in their instructions to **online** learners, and to indicate precisely the location of resources, methods of study and expectations of standards. A further concern is that the technology should not become a barrier to learning and should in fact provide additional resources for learners.

It is natural that progressive attempts to develop **open learning**, and to provide educational resources that allow for more **flexible learning**, have included a structured re-thinking of assessment techniques to ensure that each assessment actually tests what its designers think that it is testing. This would include a mix of assessment types that allows learners to capitalise on their strengths and address their weaknesses e.g. a learner who has difficulty in presenting a clear written explanation may perform better at a verbal assessment. One solution that has been adopted widely in order to work with rather than against the technology, has been the design of **blended learning** solutions in order to fit different types of learning needs to a range of technologies and pedagogies. This has the additional advantage of creating a wide variety of different types of assessment, from straight essays or reports, to varieties of online presentation on the **VLE** or by **videoconferencing**. Most forms of assessment focus on the individual performance of learners and this can be automated **multiple-choice** type tests in some forms of **CBT** or other forms of computer marked assessments (**CMA**) as opposed to tutor marked assessments (**TMA**).

Some forms of assessment emphasise **groupwork** and/or team performance as important skills to acquire for later life, and marks are awarded for the level and quality of the role of each team member as well as for the result of the group process. More recently there has been a recognition of the value of **interaction** online, both to give support to learners but also to facilitate **peer-to-peer** learning exchanges. This in turn has resulted in some online courses allocating a proportion of the marks towards learners' overall grade to reflect the quality, regularity and consistency of their online contribution, e.g. the messages **posted** on a module **discussion board** as part of a structured dialogue between tutors and learners. A further development has been the recognition by some course designers that learners can compile an **eportfolio** containing a variety of different types of assessment in order to truly reflect the skills/abilities of the learner. As in so many other aspects of education, care needs to be taken not to over-assess the learner as this often results in a shallow form of learning in order to pass specific aspects of the course rather than a deeper comprehension of information-gathering, problem-solving and critical analysis.

Finally, there is almost universal agreement that the value of all types of assessment is significantly enhanced by the quality and speed of feedback given to learners on their work.

ASYNCHRONOUS LEARNING

The term is used to describe the use of the **internet** for access to a learning environment at times and locations to suit the user. It is most commonly applied to **online** discussion groups in which messages from students and **tutors** build up over an extended period. The advantage is primarily flexibility in being able to fit learning around other commitments, but a major educational outcome is the time for reflection between **postings** and the opportunity to refine messages before posting. It has been likened to an extended seminar in which students learn from each other with the guidance of the tutor. Asynchronous learning can be contrasted with **interactivity** that is **synchronous**.

ATTACHMENT

This is usually a larger piece of writing, an image, or some other form of electronic file that is sent along with a shorter, explanatory **email** message. A common use is where a computer file containing some piece of reference material needs to be sent to several members of a group. The attachment could, of course, be sent as a **post** to online **communities** or a course **discussion board**, but could also simply be sent attached to a short email to two or three relevant people. While text might be sent by cutting-and-pasting into the body of an email message, using an attachment has the advantage of retaining the original format and style, as well as appearing tidier to the reader. It is common for images and maps etc to be sent as **jpeg** or **gif** or **pdf** attachments that would be difficult to include within the body of an email text. It is of course necessary that the recipient of the attachment has the same **software** that the sender used in order to ensure the **accessibility** of the attached file and allow it to be viewed.

AUDIO/VIDEO CLIPS

Short files containing sound and/or video images that can be sent between users either as an **attachment** to an **email**, or by means of a **hyperlink** connecting it to a relevant **webpage**. Sound and video clips are frequently used in elearning as a way to add richness to the learning experience, i.e. rather than just using text to encourage the **motivation** of the learner, and to provide an addition element of **interaction** between the **tutor** and the learner in a remote location. Simple examples might include an audio/video clip that is placed on the **VLE** and accompanies a powerpoint presentation on a certain topic. The learner can step through the powerpoint slides to the accompaniment of the voice of the tutor, talking through the presentation and explaining key points. Video clips not only provide the semblance of some social contact for learners (contrast with textual **emoticons**) but offer opportunities to demonstrate moving objects, such as engine parts, or chemistry experiments, in a controlled environment. Their use in learning activities has been somewhat restricted until recently due to the fact that both image and sound files can require a very large memory allocation for any substantial piece of recording, and consequently cause problems for users attempting to **download** and run any of these clips on a home computer. The increasing popularity and availability of **broadband** links to the **internet** is likely to overcome this difficulty for some users, although users with narrower **bandwidth** may continue to make use of **learning centres**. The need to be inclusive of students with varying levels of **ICT** access means that the **course design** of online learning resources will still require careful consideration as to when and how audio and video clips are incorporated in course resources.

AUDIOCONFERENCE

A form of many-to-many communication that utilises the telephone as a communication medium, used both for **tutor**-to-students discussion as well as for **peer-to-peer** collaboration. Unlike a **videoconference** it uses a relatively simple form of technology that most people are comfortable using in everyday life, though of course it lacks the visual impact of the videoconference. The basic method is for the tutor (or chairperson) to arrange a mutually convenient time to link all the participants together on a synchronous telephone call, working to a pre-circulated agenda or discussion topic. Depending on the telecom provider used, participants either dial into a particular conference-code number, or are dialled automatically ahead of the pre-arranged time by the operator. In common with videoconferences, **discussion boards**, and other methods of remote conferencing, the use of audioconference facilities requires a certain level of self-discipline and etiquette for the conduct of meetings.

Due to the fact that participants are not able to see body language or other visual clues, the chairperson, or **moderator**, needs to repeatedly check that other participants are a) still connected and b) understanding the content of the discussions. Simply asking a question such as, 'Does everybody understand/agree?' is more likely to cause confusion as participants, not knowing if the question is directed to themselves, are likely either to remain silent, or all speak at the same time. For this reason it is necessary to be specific in targeting questions and comments, as well as the usual vigilance needed to discourage over-dominant speakers and encourage participation from quieter members of the meeting.

There is a long history of the use of audioconference facilities in the delivery of distance learning and as a means of engaging with students who are relatively remote (in geography and/or time) from their tutor, and the technique is commonly used well in combination with other learning resources in what is now being described as **blended learning**, or as one particular tool in the design of **distributed education**. The method has quite a high level of flexibility for delivering support to students who are learning from sites other than a central campus. For example, a tutor can conduct a discussion on a particular theme with two students or twenty (usually around twelve participants, for no longer than half an hour at a time, is ideal); participants can be contacted at home, work, or even on the move; conferences can be at any mutually convenient time or day; and calls can be recorded or used in (**synchronous** or **asynchronous**) combination with other learning resources, such as printed materials, workbooks, **webpages**, or learning resources on a managed **learning environment**, to produce a very rich learning experience. Audioconferencing may experience something of a renaissance as it becomes easier to phone directly from the users' computer, using applications such as **Skype** or other **voice-over-internet** forms of **software**, and to combine this with a **VLE**, on-screen presentations, video **graphics** or other **animations**.

AUTHENTICATION

The process by which a computer system attempts to verify that a user is entitled to access a computer or a **network**, usually by a unique combination of user identification, **password** and **ISP** address when a user **logs on** to a computer. The authentication process gives the appropriate users access through the network **firewall**, to an environment of **trust** (such as a **VLE, MLE** or other online **community**) and is designed to ensure that only approved users get access to secure areas of the network.

AVATAR

Derived from a Hindu concept, in computing terms an avatar is a virtual representation of a human body. Its use is mainly confined to onscreen representation of the players in online **games**, who can be manipulated by instructions from the players and thus interact with other players via *their* avatar. In general terms it is any virtual representation of a sentient being in an **online** environment, and could include humans or animals in other forms of online interactive media such as telepresence meetings and/or some forms of interactive **videoconferencing**.

BANDWIDTH

A measure of the amount of information that can flow through an information channel communicating data between computers. Bandwidth is commonly measured in bits of information per second, with higher bandwidth facilities (**broadband**) allowing transmission of a greater volume of data, with greater speed and accuracy. A **modem** connection to an internet **server** is a typical example of a low-bandwidth connection; an Ethernet connection within a Local Area **Network** is an example of a high-bandwidth connection. Higher bandwidth transmissions allow a greater versatility in the design of **courseware**, enabling design teams to incorporate not simply large, complex files such as book chapters or reports, but also **audio/video clips** and graphical **animations**. The combination of text, sound and moving images can be used to demonstrate practical learning activities such as laboratory experiments, moving engine parts, or simulated field trips. Care needs to be taken when designing course materials for high

bandwidth users because, though the effects can be stunning and produce a rich learning environment, the inability of low bandwidth users
to **download** or view the resources frequently results in frustration and
a consequent lack of student **retention**. Low bandwidth connections
commonly result in long delays to transmit and receive information,
particularly large files and **webpages**.

BIT/BYTE

In computing, a byte is a collection of eight bits, each bit being a single
piece of digital information i.e. a 1 or a 0 denoting on or off. The only
context where elearners are likely to encounter the term with any relevance is in relation to descriptions of large files that are sent as an
attachment to **email** or messages to a **discussion board** e.g. a kilobit
(Kb) is one thousand bits, a Megabit (Mb) is one million bits, and a
Gigabit (Gb) is one thousand million bits.

BLACKBOARD

This is a commercial **VLE** (or, more strictly, **MLE**) that has become
very popular due to the clarity of its presentation and simplicity to use.
As can be seen from the **screen dump** below, the main sections are
accessed by **hyperlink** buttons, and **tutors** are able to **upload** and store
a variety of learning resources to make them available for learners to
browse and/or **download**. There are separate sections for assignments,
course documents, communications, and other tools (including **dropbox**). Other popular MLE include **WebCT** as well as **open source**
environments such as customised variants of Boddington and Moodle.
Blackboard and WebCT are now set to merge, and it is interesting to
speculate on the possible **convergence** of other major brands as elearning expands to become a mainstream element of all levels of educational
provision.

BLENDED LEARNING

The term blended learning became popular around 2000 and is now
widely used in North America, the UK and Australia, and in academic as
well as training circles. The original and still most common meaning

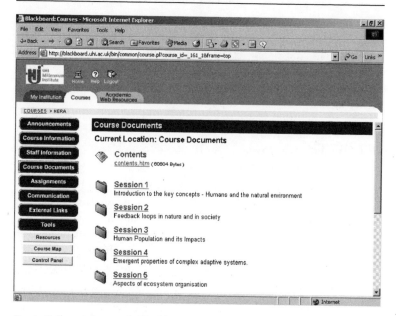

Figure 3 Screen dump of a Blackboard site

refers to combinations of **online** and **face-to-face** (**f2f**) teaching. However, other combinations of technologies, locations or pedagogical approaches are increasingly being identified as examples of blended learning. For example:

- Where both **synchronous** and **asynchronous** technologies are used on an online course;
- Where combinations of formal and informal learning are used in workplace professional development;
- Where students are accessing course material and resources from a variety of locations – home, **learning centre**, college etc;
- Where technology is used to redesign high enrolment courses to enhance quality and reduce costs.

In reality, any course or even any learning experience almost inevitably involves a combination of different inputs: reading, thinking, writing and talking to peers or **tutors**. Consequently, as the use of the term widens, it becomes less and less useful as a descriptor. Critics have come to the fore to claim that 'blended learning' is simply a new label that is being applied to old goods but, although this may be true, it neglects to consider two important elements. First, in historical terms, online learning is a new mode of learning opportunity, and it has the potential to fundamentally alter the relationship between the learner and the tutor. How this blend is able to mature and combine the best aspects of both 'conventional' and online media is as yet an unfinished chapter. It is therefore rather early to dismiss experimental combinations of different learning blends that incorporate new technology as simply a marketing gimmick. Second, even if 'blended learning' is simply a new label on a method of education that tutors have been practicing for several decades, the fact that it has now been recognised as a legitimate, even desirable, approach to educational resource delivery has profound implications for the ways in which we embark upon course construction.

Recent research purports to show that blended learning is more effective and students learn more and enjoy it more than on either face-to-face or online teaching alone (see http://www.learningcircuits.org/2003/jul2003/rossett.htm). Blended learning is said to combine the power and effectiveness of the classroom with the flexibility and any-time nature of elearning and allows learning to be more tailored and more individualistic, whilst at the same time allowing greater reach and distributed delivery. Without getting into the eternal debate of 'teaching versus learning' the strong implications of the term 'blended learning' are that:

a) diverse opportunities to present learning resources and ways of communication between tutor-student and student-student are more flexible and more desirable than narrower, one-track solutions;
b) individual learners will, if encouraged to play an active part in their own educational development, select learning resources from different media and sources that are more convenient and appropriate for their personal situation. This might include the alternative option (or replacement) of lectures with **webcasts** or recorded CDs, of live discussions with asynchronous online discussion, of targeted, digitised articles in the absence of a nearby university library with thousands of books, or the provision of structured reading lists that link to online academic journals.

The questions that are repeatedly asked about blended learning centre around what is the best blend? Is one blend more effective than another? So far there is little evidence from which to generalise, but many educators and trainers seem to conclude that the answers lie in a cultural shift away from teaching and training, and toward learning and the **motivation** of learners. A significant preoccupation for course designers and educational analysts is how to intentionally design the optimum blended

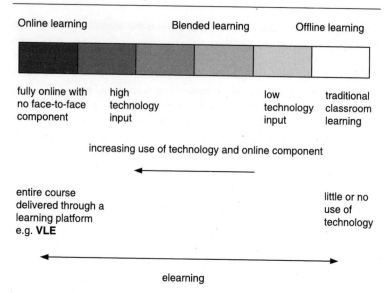

Figure 4 A schematic description of blended learning
Source: An introduction to elearning: Using the NLN materials within a Virtual Learning Environment (JISC, 2003) (Re-drawn by Fiona Rennie)

learning course, rather than allow historical circumstance, chance and individual tutor biases to dictate the mixture of the final blend. This approach stresses diversity in the development of learning materials, **courseware, assessments** and supporting resources, and is becoming synonymous with **distributed education**, although the latter also has strong geographical implications.

An alternative though much less common term is hybrid learning.

Further reading

Bonk, C. and Graham, C. (2005). *The Handbook of Blended Learning.* Pfeiffer Wiley.
Dean, P., Stahl, M., Sylwester, D., and Pear, J. (2001). Effectiveness of combined delivery modalities for distance learning and resident learning. *Quarterly Review Of Distance Education*, 2(3), 247–254.

BLOGGING (WEBLOGGING)

A weblog, web log or simply a blog, is a **web** application which contains periodic time-stamped **posts** on a common **webpage.** These posts are often but not necessarily in reverse chronological order. Blogs are usually written by a single author, rather like a diary, but occasionally they are group activities with many authors. Most weblogs enable visitors to leave public comments, which can lead to a community of readers centered around the blog; others are non-interactive.

A blog is and has always been more than the **online** equivalent of a personal journal. The blog adds to the form of the diary by incorporating the best features of **hypertext**: the capacity to link to new and useful resources. But a blog is also characterised by its use of a personal style, and this style may be reflected in either the writing or the selection of links passed along to readers. Blogs are, in their purest form, the core of what has come to be called personal publishing. What makes blogs so attractive, in both the educational community and the **internet** at large, is their ease of use. A blog owner can edit or update a new entry without worrying about page formats or **HTML** syntax.

Educators are still in the experimental phase of understanding the value of this medium. There is little doubt that as an educational process, regular blogging develops a range of skills such as: **information literacy**, critical thinking, writing and self-expression skills. What is more significant is that it offers students a chance to reflect on what they are writing and thinking, and to do this over a sustained period of time. If comments by other students are encouraged, the student is writing for an audience of peers and can learn the art of engaging readers in a sustained conversation.

However, when blogging is used by teachers in a prescriptive way, such as, 'write a blog on the subject of XXX', the value of blogging is very much constrained and it becomes another writing exercise. As many writers have noted, blogging is, at its best, a conversation and needs a purpose and an audience, but not prescribed topics.

Blogging **software** breaks down into two major categories: hosting services and installed applications. A hosting service is a **website** that will give you access to everything you need in order to create a blog. It will offer a form for you to input your entries, some tools that allow you to create a template for your blog, and access to some built-in accessories. A remotely installed application is a piece of software that you obtain from the provider and install on your own website. These systems are similar to web-based applications such as ColdFusion or Hypermail. Because of this, the number of users is much lower, but those who do use them tend (arguably) to be more dedicated and more knowledgeable than those who use hosting services. Installed applications are also more suitable for institutional use, since access can be controlled.

Some educators choose to use specific weblog software instead of traditional course management tools, such as **WebCT, Blackboard** and others, due to the closed nature of the latter. These educators may prefer that their course content be openly available and shareable with colleagues. They may also want discussions or student work to be carried over and available after a specific course ends. Weblogs are not closed environments and allow content to remain after a course ends. It is also possible to use weblog content within WebCT and Blackboard. This provides many interesting options for educators, including adding dynamic content to a course and sharing content across multiple courses within a degree programme.

Blogging is also a useful tool for teachers. They can use it to build an archive of readings and research resources. They can share their reflections on research or pedagogy with colleagues, and use it for instant publishing of ideas, innovations or other results.

In organisations, blogging is being used as a knowledge management tool. It works well as a way of disseminating tacit rather than explicit information. In this regard, some commentators note the similarities of blogging with storytelling. Stories convey understanding because they are told in context. Context conveys emotions, triggers individual and group memories, provides intuition and insights to events. Bloggers establish context over an extended period of time and since their audience is usually made of regular visitors, context can be implied or can be explicitly **hyperlinked** to a previous entry.

Despite these indications, there is general agreement that trying to define precisely what blogging is actually about, is an exercise in futility, because blogs are constantly shifting, evolving and becoming something else.

Those who have been involved in elearning since the beginning will notice a similarity in these comments about blogging to earlier promotions of **computer conferencing**, and before that, of **email**. Similar learning benefits are common to all: **interaction**, communication, reflection, wide audience, opportunity for **feedback** and refining ideas, archiving and re-reading possibilities, and so on. What makes blogging better or different than computer conferencing? Students who have used both say that blogging is more personal and sustained, that it offers a better opportunity to build expertise, and in the end that it is more fun!

Web links

http://www.corporateblogging.info/2005/03/learning-blogosphere.asp
http://www.educause.edu/ir/library/pdf/erm0450.pdf
http://www.criticalmethods.org/collab/v.mv?d=1_40

BLUETOOTH

A type of wireless radio communications standard that enables secure, low-cost signals to be exchanged between devices such as personal computers, mobile phones, laptops and personal digital assistants (PDAs). The standard is ideal for mobile users who need to communicate with a **network** to exchange information. It is designed to be used with devices which have low power consumption, and will allow the devices to exchange information automatically when they come within range (usually a few tens of metres) They are ideal for **wireless networks** and have been used, for example, within small confined areas such as an open-plan office to communicate between the mouse and the computer, or the computer and a printer.

BRAINSTORMING

Is a method of generating ideas amongst a group of learners. It works well in an elearning context as students can add ideas over time. The two key elements are: defining the problem or idea and establishing an environment in which anything related to the topic can be contributed without criticism or rejection. It can operate either formally or informally with a large or small group.

BROADBAND

Broadband is the method of sending and receiving data over high-speed **networks**. It is most commonly associated with a far faster way of connecting a computer to the **internet** than is possible through a conventional dial up method, which uses standard telephone networks. Broadband connections that use cable or ADSL mean there is greater capacity to send data than via standard telephone networks. This means that far more information can be transmitted in the same period of time than a conventional dial up connection – allowing faster viewing of **webpages**, faster downloading of files and faster access to **email**.

Broadband-supported learning offers a means to facilitate the introduction of innovative approaches to teaching and learning that privilege collaboration, shared knowledge construction, peer-to-peer **interaction** and **mentoring** unrestricted by geographic, cultural or temporal barriers.

Broadband is fundamentally changing the way research is conducted in the higher education sector. Researchers rely heavily on the internet to access research information and online journals, and to communicate with colleagues overseas. There is growing use of modelling and data visualisation in research to better understand complex processes, especially in fields such as environmental science and biotechnology. Such research is dependent on the availability of high performance computing and advanced networks to facilitate the manipulation and exchange of very large data sets. Those universities that lack sufficient **bandwidth** will increasingly find that they are unable to participate in key fields of research.

Newer technologies like wireless, mobile and broadband will increase immeasurably the possible blends for both campus-based and distance education. Mobile devices, such as Personal Digital Assistants (PDAs), mobile phones, wireless laptops and tablet PCs, are being introduced into courses to increase flexibility, widen participation, allow more natural interaction and collaboration, and to use handwriting rather than keyboarding. Broadband, or high speed internet access, bring a number of advantages to the education sector: speed, 'always-on' convenience and **multimedia** communication. At its simplest, high speed internet access will allow the sort of fast response **download** and rapid **peer-to-peer** interaction that campus-based users in universities and corporate business have been used to for some time. Broadband is already blurring the divide between **face-to-face** (**f2f**) and online students, the more so as campus-based courses increasingly incorporate levels of online interaction in their learning plans.

BROWSER

A shorthand term for a '**web** browser'. This is a **software** application that allows users to access and interact with a **search engine** that is hosted on a **server** in order to view **webpages** that are written in **HTML**. Browsers that are currently popular include Internet Explorer, Firefox and Netscape.

BULLETIN BOARD SYSTEM (BBS)

Bulletin boards are an early form of electronic messaging **software** that allows the user to send and receive messages and **upload** and **download** files. BBS are text-based and usually serve a specific community. They tend to be used for exchanging software and for chatting, rather than for formal educational discussions. In the United States alone, there are tens of thousands of BBSs.

CASE STUDY

The case study method has a long tradition in the teaching of law, business and medicine. Recently its use has spread to other areas of the curriculum and particularly to an elearning context. Case studies are often used to demonstrate effective practice and to illustrate general principles through specific examples. In the UK, JISC, the Joint Information Systems Committee, has devised a template to collect, document and disseminate case studies across the UK Higher Education community.

Figure 5 was developed by JISC as part of the Pedagogy Strand of the JISC e-Learning Programme. More information at www.jisc.ac.uk/ elearning_pedagogy.html for the strand and www.jisc.ac.uk/ elp_practice.html for more information on the case studies developed as part of the Effective Practice with eLearning guide.

CHATROOM/CHATBOX

A simple form of computer mediated communication (**CMC**) that allows users to participate in **synchronous** communication with each other, usually in the form of short **text messages**. The synchronicity distinguishes it from a **discussion board**, which is usually **asynchronous**. Most chatrooms are dedicated to particular themes or topics of common interest, and in this respect they could be considered small, temporary **communities** that are **online**. Some chatrooms may allow the users to represent themselves with an **avatar**, but mostly they are restricted to simple text communications, and users are required to include **emoticons** in order to convey emotions such as anger or humour. The limitations of the demands for synchronous access and the superficiality of many of the chatrooms have limited their potential for elearning, but they are still popular among teenagers and certain elements of the **games and gaming** community. Concern over opportunities for child abuse has led to a **password** protection system on most school chatroom facilities, but in this manner they can offer a fun and safe way to introduce children to the world of online communications.

Case study title	
Institution name	
Background [Give brief details of institution, type of learners and learning environment in which the activity/ies took place]	
Intended outcome(s) [Describe the objective(s) behind the practice outlined here]	
The challenge [Identify the issues that required attention or which prompted you to re-assess your previous practice]	
Established practice [Identify features of the practice previously in use - this may include any aspects which were subsequently amended]	
The e-learning advantage [Describe the benefits of the addition or amendment of an element of e-learning, as experienced by learners, practitioners and/or the institution as a whole]	
Key points for effective practice [Briefly identify the most important points in the case study for other practitioners - these may include risks as well as benefits]	
Conclusions and recommendations [A summary of how and why the practice outlined here has been effective]	
Additional information [Use this optional section to add related materials or content e.g. a lesson plan or a set of data, or to supply your email address]	

Figure 5 Template for case studies descriptions

CLIENT

This is a computer system that is able to access a remote service on another computer via computer **networks** that are connected by the **internet**. Common examples are the client **software** that we use to retrieve our **email** from the memory of the **server** that our internet service provider (**ISP**) operates for us; or the client **browser** that we use to access and read **webpages**. It is becoming common practice that when new elearners begin a course, they will be sent appropriate client software by their educational establishment to **upload** to their home/ work computer in order that the learner can access educational resources and communications tools to aid their studies.

CMA

A Computer Marked Assignment (as opposed to a **TMA**). The general idea is that for some subjects and at some levels of study, it is possible to construct a range of questions for which there is only one best answer, (sometimes called **multiple-choice-questions – MCQ**). As a result, the completed assignment has no subjective elements, and can be marked by a computer. Initially learners selected their choice of answer by entering a pencil mark in an appropriate box, which was then passed through an optical scanner and 'read' by a computer. The creation of interactive **webpages** has meant that learners can go **online**, work through a list of questions making their selection, and receive almost immediate **feedback** on their choice. The web-based environment allows a variety of resources such as text, sound and images to be used, and the automated nature of the CMA structure is especially useful with large numbers of learners. Although the short response may limit the depth to which knowledge is tested, CMAs are frequently included in **elearning courses** as short self-test formative **assessments** to provide immediate feedback to learners on their progress.

CMC

Computer Mediated Conferencing, or a synonym for **computer conferencing**.

COLLABORATIVE WORK/LEARNING

The practice of collaborative work or collaborative learning amongst **online** educators is widespread. It has spawned its own acronym: **CSCW** or CSCL which stand for Computer Supported Collaborative Work or Learning. The definition of the term as applied to elearning is: work jointly carried out on an activity or project to gain knowledge or skills. In some respects online collaborative activities bring together the unique and most valued attributes of elearning:

- communication and **interaction** amongst peers;
- structured learning devised by the course designer(s);
- access to the resources of the **internet**;
- opportunity for students to develop team working skills;
- learning by doing;
- small group activity.

The size of the group and the length of time allowed for the activity are issues that need to be tailored to the individual context. A typical example of a collaborative activity in a distributed higher education situation where the students do not meet would be: a group of five to seven with two to three weeks to complete the activity. Examples of collaborative activities would include: an online debate; constructing a website on one of the course topics; writing a joint review of the best websites on a relevant topic, or of some specified journal articles.

The way in which the group works has been the subject of some discussion in the elearning literature. In particular, collaborative work has been distinguished from cooperative work. Where the group decides to split the work according to existing skills and assemble the different parts at the end, cooperative work is operating. The participants cooperate, but they take on the part of the task they can already do. In collaborative work, there is more negotiation, commenting and sharing. The learning comes from the process of interacting, reflecting and collaborating on how to do the task. In collaborative learning students give and receive help from their peers; they exchange resources and information; they challenge each other and jointly reflect on their progress. In short, collaborative activities develop team working skills amongst the group through focusing on a common goal. In this way, collaboration helps to overcome some of the ill effects of competition that is the mainstay of much formal education.

There are a number of barriers to elearning through collaborative activities. First of all, it can be very time-consuming. Negotiating tasks in an **asynchronous**, distance learning environment can be difficult, especially when no one wants to assume the leadership role. One way of speeding up the process, at least in the early stage of the course, is for the **tutor** to assign roles. This reduces the experience of negotiation for students, but the aim would be for students to negotiate roles themselves in the next activity. The fact is that most students have more experience of competing with each other than with collaborating, so this skill needs to be developed over time.

A second problem is inherent with all forms of collaboration whether online or offline: participants contributing unequally. This becomes particularly contentious if the collaborative activity is part of the **assessment** of the course. Some tutors give one mark to everyone in the group. Others have devised a system whereby students grade each others' work, sometimes including a self mark as well as a tutor mark. Yet another alternative is an assignment in which part of the work is collaboratively produced and the other part is individual (e.g. an introduction and summary written separately by each student). This means that the student receives an individual mark made up of the group collaborative mark plus the mark for the student's own work.

Collaborative activities require good design skills on the part of the tutor(s). Finding topics and collaborative processes that work well in a particular discipline needs practice and experimentation. Equally critical to the success of collaborative working is the quality of **tutoring**: knowing when to intervene and how much to contribute are again skills that are only acquired through experience. Some tutors start off the activity and do not intervene at all until the end when they perhaps provide a summary or overview of the collaborative process. Others keep a close watch on the interactions and are ready to intervene if they think the collaboration is floundering. They might **email** individual students to suggest a way forward or a contribution they might make. Or they might add comments to the collaboration space to try to model how the students might interact. Occasionally tutors will invite or assign students to take on the tutor's role in order to develop leadership skills in the group.

Another difficulty with online collaboration, compared with **face-to-face (f2f)** collaboration, is the reticence students feel about contradicting or challenging each other to explain what they mean. This is undoubtedly due to the lack of visual clues in the online environment and as students become more comfortable interacting online, they tend to become more assertive. Nevertheless, the tutor needs to encourage students to challenge ideas through modelling this process in response to students' messages.

Online collaborative work usually takes place through asynchronous discussion. However, it is possible and can be beneficial to include some **synchronous** discussions. Technologies for synchronous interaction include: text chat, shared screen plus text chat, and full **audioconference** and **videoconference**. Synchronous interaction provides immediate **feedback**, so can help with negotiations. Social processes are also important for successful collaboration and a synchronous session can provide greater social presence than the asynchronous environment.

There is a range of websites or **portals** about collaborative learning. A particularly good one geared for higher education is Australian (see below for **URL**) because it contains a large number of online articles, journals and books about collaborative learning, a series of guest editorials and a section on technologies to support online collaboration. A site for the school sector is the Global SchoolNet Foundation which has been operating since 1984 to link school children around the world for joint projects.

Web links

http://clp.cqu.edu.au/
http://www.globalschoolnet.org/index.html

COMMUNITIES

The term 'virtual communities' has increasingly been applied to communication **networks** in which the participants are not located in the same geographical place, but are distributed across the globe. Unfortunately the term seems to have almost as many definitions and descriptions as the 'traditional' communities of place, and arguments still emerge as to what is and is not an **online** community. An online community is a social network that uses computer support as the basis of communication among members instead of **face-to-face (f2f)** interaction. Two crucial aspects in the development of interactive learning networks, whether online or on-site, are the swift establishment of **trust** between the participants, and the development of **collaborative** learning activities. These collaborative activities may include small groups of students reading material on different topics and preparing summaries for the rest of the class, as well as debates, group projects, **role play**, and collaborative essays, **case studies**, or research plans.

A key feature to recognise is that in the development of this type of interactive network, the community of learners, becomes the learning network, as much as the computer-based communications system that supports it. Critics of the social value of online communities maintain that online communication, such as **email**, creates the sensation of being part of a community of people, interacting for the common good, but is substantially an illusion. This is difficult to counter, for two main reasons, first the complex and diverse interactions that take place in 'real' communities of place are not fully understood and many are contested by academics (e.g. we appear to regard our regular network of telephone contacts, or our superficial but regular contacts made through our work as real communities although we do not reside together.) Second, the scope and depth of online contacts is so wide, from the occasional email inquiry from a friend-of-a-friend, to active many-to-many academic discussion lists, to the detailed collaborative information sharing on groove networks, or other shared work spaces, that it seems foolish and irresponsible to catalogue all online relationships as illusory or superficial. While it is true that electronic communications (phone, **videoconferences**, email and shared **desktops**) create the illusion of proximity between participants, the question is whether proximity is a mandatory requirement for a community, or whether in this instance, the liberating results of technology have allowed us to ameliorate, if not remove, the tyranny of distance.

Though most early sociological work related to the concept of community as a physical territory where residents interact, there was also a contrasting view of community as an interactional field held together by the human need to interact with other human beings. The **internet** can be used to create abstract places (virtual offices, **online libraries**, online work spaces, and spaces for **peer-to-peer** interactive **games**), representations of the self (online identities), and abstract interactions (with other identities and with automated tasks), but it is this latter view of community which has come to be applied to online social networks.

At the very least a community seems to be distinguished by a shared understanding of its boundaries, whether these are geographical, or defined by particular areas of common interest. Common activities help to create a sense of community by providing a common sense of identity with which the members of the community can associate themselves.

It may be useful to think of community as both the outcome and the context of informal networking, with the 'well-connected community' being achieved when people feel part of a web of diverse and interlocking relationships.

In both communities of place and online communities, it is important to understand that networking is a vital component of community development practice because it creates the conditions for robust, yet flexible forms of collective action. A key community-building element resulting from social networking is the fostering of **trust** between the members of the network. Through the sheer number and speed of possible connections, the **web** has emerged as a powerful new technological vehicle for harvesting the personal experiences of others and the construction of tools that attempt to make this collective activity more visible (and accessible) is a major research field. The fact that these connections can be somewhat distant, impersonal, and even largely anonymous (the user shares only what s/he wants to share) can be a strength as well as an obstacle to elearning.

Simply because an online community has a less tangible physical presence (because the community is dispersed and may never meet face-to-face) does not negate its existence. A useful comparison might be made with our references to the political 'sphere of influence' in which subtle civic and political communications and allegiances may operate without a face-to-face network of players. Similarly the social construction made by economists called 'the market' to describe the local or global interplay of economic processes involving supply and demand is not weakened because there is no physical market-place where all the participants can sit down **face-to-face** (**f2f**) to negotiate their complex deals. The invention of the 'virtual community' as a term to describe computer networked interactions is not consistent if it is not also applied to earlier forms of distributed interactive networks. It was a useful term to give a shorthand description of the exciting and rapid appearance of a wider range of global connections through computer mediated communications, but on closer analysis, with more persistent usage, the term has become an over-used, redundant and misleading appellation.

This sense of community is derived from the participants' perception of being linked into a complex system of relationships and interaction, and these shared experiences help to foster group solidarity and a sense of common purpose. Online communities have been roughly classified into five different types:

1. Communities of purpose, formed by people who are trying to achieve a similar objective, who assist each other by sharing experiences, information and **peer-to-peer** knowledge.
2. Communities of practice, formed by groups of people sharing a similar profession or vocation who seek to share experiences and facilitate professional exchange (which may also add value to offline networks).
3. Communities of circumstance, which are similar to communities of

practice but are generally more personally focused, or related to life experiences, and not driven by professional activities.

4. Communities of interest, linking people who share their ideas, passion and knowledge in a common interest or theme, but might know very little about each other outside this shared interest.

5. Communities of users, who are represented by the more innovative and interactive business networks that allow customer-to-customer exchanges, including the sharing of information, reviews and specific themed discussions.

In an increasingly electronically networked world we may occupy more than one of these communities at different times of our day, working, learning and socialising. Online groups have the ability to connect with their community of interest at any time of day or night to share information or solicit help, and it is common that online relationships also move to include other forms of communication, e.g. telephone, post and/or face-to-face interaction.

We can list three key criteria that define successful online communities:

1. Self-generated evolution, where members of the community generate the content for the site, and take decisions to influence its growth, adaptation and evolution.

2. Involvement and interactivity, through which members participate and interact with other members of the community (e.g. through email, **bulletin boards, synchronous** chat etc.)

3. Frequency and duration of visits, that encourage members to come back to the site repeatedly in order to share their ideas with other community members as part of the process of establishing a collective identity and sense of trust between members of the community.

There is a clear indication that the participants in online communities are not attracted to them by the provision of tools alone, but need to be able to recognise a common bond with other members of that community. It is this shared set of experiences which provides the potent stimulant of learning opportunities. According to this, the true function of a community is to provide an agreed regulation, discipline and a conduit for self-expression that is consistent with the greater good of the participant group as a whole. A key mechanism for achieving this is through fostering social institutions, which extends the concept of community beyond clusters of like-minded enthusiasts in common interest groups, to networks of distinct but independent institutions.

These heterogeneous networks differentiate the framework of a community from its constituent, narrower, common interest groups.

Further reading

Gongla, P. and Rizzuto, C. R. 2001. Evolving communities of practice: IBM Global Services experience. *IBM Systems Journal*, 40 (4), 842–862. URL: http://www.research.ibm.com/journal/sj/404/gongla.html

Kim, A. J. 2000. *Community building on the Web: secret strategies for successful online communities*. Berkeley, CA, USA: Peachpit Press. ISBN 0–201–87484–9.

Preece, J. 2000. *Online Communities: Designing Usability. Supporting Sociability*. Chichester: Wiley. ISBN 0–471–80599–8.

COMPUTER-BASED TRAINING (CBT)

Computer-Based Training is a term commonly used in corporate training circles, whereas CAI, Computer-Assisted Instruction was the comparable term in education. With the advent of the **web**, both terms are passing out of use. CBT is usually a stand-alone package for training employees in company processes or in computer skills. Most packages contain tests, often **multiple choice questionnaires**, and the results may be logged so that the employee cannot progress without passing. The main limitation of CBT is that it is costly and time-consuming to produce, especially when **graphics** or **animations** are included. For large training requirements with a relatively unchanging subject matter, CBT may still be cost effective. Many computers contain short CBT sequences for users to learn about the facilities it offers. The term 'computer-based learning' (CBL) is also sometimes used in elearning, especially for the provision of extra 'remedial' tutorials in difficult areas e.g. maths or statistics.

COMPUTER CONFERENCING

The terms computer conferencing and the similar **CMC**, computer-mediated communication, are early words for what is now called elearning. As these terms pre-date the **web**, they largely concerned the communications side of **online** learning, **Software** which integrates online content and communication only became prevalent with **VLEs**. Consequently, literature referring to computer conferencing focuses on the kind of software that facilitates textual **interactions** amongst students and the **tutor**, on the **asynchronous** nature of the communication and on the impact on the evolving conversation created by the opportunity for reflection. The novelty of this kind of interaction has largely ceased to be the focus of research, although many researchers continue to study the processes, the pedagogical value and the success of online communication.

The reasons for teachers introducing computer conferencing remain unchanged:

- students are distributed geographically;
- the demand for more flexible offerings;
- the perceived advantages of **blended learning**;
- the need for students to develop **ICT** skills.

The limitations of the medium for education are also fundamentally unchanged, although VLEs have increased the potential for more varied forms of communication e.g. **synchronous** interaction, **video and audio clips, blogging** and **instant messaging**. Nevertheless, the experience of discussing academic issues through text is challenging to learners accustomed only to **face-to-face (f2f)** interaction. The lack of visual and physical presence is something that a minority of learners find hard to accept, and never seem to regard textual communication as a vehicle for learning. Asynchronous online **interaction** can also be time-consuming, both for the tutor and the students. Busy students who have to fit their studying around employment, family and other responsibilities often find that online interaction is not an efficient use of their limited time. Moreover, computer conferencing does not demand their attention in the way that more immediate life situations do; consequently, logging on to the online discussion can easily be pushed to the bottom of their list of things to do. This leads to the feeling of guilt and frustration which many students of online courses report.

The way in which computer conferencing is integrated into the rest of the course is critical to its successful use. If the use is marginal, or perceived by students to be optional, the strategic learners will focus their efforts on the essential elements of the course and **log on** rarely or not at all. It is particularly difficult (though not impossible) to develop rich and pedagogically valuable discussions when students see each other regularly on campus. Structured activities and assessed online contributions are two possible solutions to successful **blended learning**.

Two issues which today are accepted as part of the medium, preoccupied early researchers of computer conferencing:

1. The perceived equality of this means of communication has been

compared with face-to-face seminars, where speakers have to wait their turn to speak. With computer conferencing all students can input messages whenever they are ready. Furthermore, the lack of visual cues puts all participants on an equal footing, regardless of colour, disability, facial characteristics or accent. Although this is true in theory, in reality students who are more articulate, who have easy online access or who want to dominate discussions still can and do. Without careful intervention by the tutor, the shy, inarticulate and less confident students can be marginalised online just as they can be face-to-face. One phenomenon which has been noted many times, however, is that the tutor does not dominate discussion online to nearly the same extent as happens in face-to-face seminars. Other researchers have noted that some students who rarely speak in face-to-face discussions take a greater part in online discussions. So while the medium does not guarantee equality of participation, it usually improves on the interaction patterns of face-to-face seminars.

2. The fact that messages in computer conferencing software are archived means that there is a **database** of interactions. Students can refer back to messages and use extracts from them in their assignments; the tutor can use the archive to write a summary of the discussion or to grade students' contributions. In general the archive distinguishes asynchronous communication from face-to-face seminars by being available rather than ephemeral.

In the past, when computer conferencing was a new phenomenon, one of the techniques used to motivate students and add focus to the discussions was to invite a guest lecturer to tutor the course for a week or two. Of course this guest expert could enter the conference from anywhere, read messages and add comments. Often the expert would begin with an opening statement or use an existing paper as a background resource to spark off the discussion. As elearning has become commonplace now, this practice is used much less frequently. The novelty of online interaction has worn off and most experts are too busy running their own courses.

Another practice which began at the outset of educational computer conferencing was the provision of a social conference, where students were free to discuss matters not related to the course. Initially the purpose was to prevent social interaction taking place in the academic discussion conferences. It soon became apparent, however, that these social spaces fulfilled a very necessary function in building community and **trust**. Through humour, chit-chat and exchanges about their personal lives, students get to know each other and develop an awareness of themselves as a group. Unlike the practice of guest lecturers, social conferences continue to be used on most online courses.

The use of **emoticons** or smileys developed very early in the history of computer conferencing, as a way of overcoming the lack of para-linguistic clues. Initially, conferencing software was command line and offered no facilities for any kind of typeface emphasis such as highlighting or emboldening. Happy, surprised and sad faces were used to provide some of this missing emphasis.

The term computer conferencing was used alongside **videoconferencing** and **audioconferencing** when all three were very distinct media. The advent of the web has led to the **convergence** of these means of communication, such that the term computer conferencing is rarely used now.

Further reading

Hiltz, S. and Goldman, R. (eds) (2005). *Learning Together Online: Research on Asynchronous Learning Networks*. New Jersey: Lawrence Erlbaum Associates.

CONSTRUCTIVISM

A theory about learning which considers that learners construct knowledge for themselves. Each learner individually constructs meaning as he or she learns. Elearning is strongly associated with constructivism as both are learner-centred rather than teacher-centred. There are a number of general principles of learning that are derived from constructivism and that are well supported through elearning:

- Learning is an active process in which the learner engages with ideas and interacts with other learners in order to construct meaning;
- Reflection on learning is another key component of constructivist theory. Learning consists both of constructing meaning and constructing systems of meaning;
- Learning involves language and self-expression. The **online** environment supports this function;
- Learning is a social activity: our learning is intimately associated with our connection with other human beings, our teacher, our peers, our family, as well as casual acquaintances;
- Learning is contextual: we learn in relationship to what else we know, what we believe, our prejudices and our fears;
- One needs knowledge to learn: it is not possible to absorb new

knowledge without having some structure developed from previous knowledge to build on. The more we know, the more we learn;

- Learning is not instantaneous: it takes time to learn. For significant learning we need to revisit ideas, ponder them, try them out, play with them and use them.

CONVERGENCE

In the context of **ICT**, this term describes the inter-operability of different forms of applications and devices which allows them to communicate with one another. The growth of convergence has been made easier as analogue technologies (e.g. magnetic-tape cassettes) have been replaced by digital sources of information. Convergence basically allows one piece of equipment or **software** to communicate with another. Examples of convergence in terms of elearning include the ability to utilise digital television or hand-held devices such as certain mobile phones for **surfing** the **internet**. Another example would be to take a picture with a digital camera that can then be **uploaded** to a laptop computer and then sent by **email** to a colleague or course **tutor**. Increasing convergence has allowed learners to communicate with their institutional **VLE** by using whatever **ISP** they choose to send email, to use mobile phones for **text messaging** to a **module bulletin board** or to stream **videoconferences** onto their own desktop PCs.

As **networks** of varied devices are created and enlarged by convergence we see a trend towards learners being able to access learning resources from all sorts of different locations (pervasive learning) or while they are on the move (mobile learning). To be most successful, the users should be unaware of the technicalities of convergence so that they are able to concentrate on using the device of their choice to communicate with another person or device without being deterred by the technology. Greater convergence allows greater flexibility in pursuing opportunities for **distributed education**, and with the spread of **wireless networks** it has become possible to link communications devices over the internet in more flexible ways than can be allowed for with fixed cabling, e.g. working on the move, or in ad hoc meetings.

COOKIE

A small file that can be sent to a computer by a **server** when a connection is made over the **internet**. When the server is contacted, e.g. when surfing the **web** for a particular product, the server sends a small file to the hard disk on the user's computer. The next time that contact is made with this server, the cookie on the user's computer is read by the server, enabling it to recognise the user and greet them by name. The information collected by the cookie can be used to gather information on individual users, and to create a user profile that can help customise individual preferences. An example might be that when a user connects to Amazon on their usual computer, the website greets the user by name and is able to recommend particular books or music that s/he might like. This is based upon a complex **database** that has recorded the previous items that the user has purchased from them, the items that s/he has **browsed**, and a comparison with the purchasing preferences of other users who have selected some of the same products. There is a considerable potential for this type of user profile creation among elearners, but restrictions of **copyright** and data protection laws currently limit its application.

COPYRIGHT

This is the complex set of legal rights that is used to control the manner in which an idea is expressed, and how the idea is replicated. Common examples include the restricted right to copy text or images from books, magazines, journals etc. The intention of copyright is to allow the 'owner' of the idea (such as a story, an explanation, or a piece of creative work) to benefit from the idea for a fixed period of time. In a digital age, copyright causes problems because it has become very much easier to replicate text digitally, change it slightly, and incorporate it in another piece of work. Copying a piece of work without acknowledging the source with a full reference is termed **plagiarism**, and can prove to be problematic to detect in an elearning environment. Although short quotations and descriptive paragraphs can normally be used freely, the replication of entire journal articles and books e.g. on a **VLE** is normally copyright restricted and requires the payment of royalties. Many educationalists have argued that copyright operates against the spirit of information being freely available on the **internet** for educational purposes and therefore that copyright is losing its value in the digital age. Attempts to circumvent the restrictions of copyright include the use of educational **portals**, that give secure access (**password** protected) to collections of **online** journals and ebooks, as well as **digitizing** selected key articles for a course (for which a copyright fee is paid) and making these electronically available to authorised learners.

CORPORATE UNIVERSITY

Corporations develop either a virtual or physical university in order to align their training and learning with their business strategy. The aim is usually to sustain or establish competitive advantage through learning, to achieve performance goals and to drive cultural transformation. The corporate university often integrates the existing training departments and sets up a governance system of senior executives to assure the corporate aims and objectives are met.

COURSE DESIGN

The design of course materials for elearning is the most crucial, but also perhaps the most contested aspect of **online** learning. On the one hand, critics have tended to dismiss elearning as a poor substitute for 'the real thing' (i.e. conventional, classroom-based education) with students simply being encouraged to search the **internet** for learning resources and with little or no **tutor** input. The use of the word 'virtual' in **VLE** and **'virtual university'** is a legacy of this thinking. On the other hand, proponents of elearning have claimed that a well-structured course can provide more contact between tutor and student than many 'conventional' courses, and that the educational experience is better because that tutor contact is applied in the context of the individual learner. Both advocates and detractors agree that good course design for elearning is more than simply giving out lecture notes and further reading suggestions by **posting** them on the **web** (although this seems still to be the case in some conventional courses!)

Thinking carefully about course design for elearning is not very different from thinking about good course design in a more traditional format, except that there are more varied forms of communication between participants, and greater diversity of formats for learning resources. The initial starting point must be a careful consideration of what it is that the tutor wants the students to have learned by the end of the **module**. These learning outcomes are then matched with appropriate types of **assessment**; following this, the design team needs to identify and select relevant sections of supporting evidence, additional reading, definitions of concepts and explanatory information that can assist the learner to acquire the appropriate level of understanding in the subject. In elearning, or in **distributed education** more generally, decisions need to be taken at this stage to select the most appropriate media, technologies and learning resources to share the different educational components with the learners. This is critical if the **ICT** resources and other media are to support the learning process rather than becoming a dominating factor in themselves. Good elearning not only captures the benefits of the **asynchronous learning** opportunities that are created, but also exploits the advantages of a diverse range of digital resources available over the internet, such as:

- **Discussion boards** and/or **chatroom** facilities to encourage dialogue with students;
- **Audio/video clips** to provide learning resources other than simple text;
- **Hyperlinks** to other sources of information such as useful **webpages**, links to **portals** and/or **online libraries**;
- Activities to promote **interaction** between learners, and between learner and tutor (either individually or in **tutor groups**);
- Opportunities for assessment, including self-assessment through activities such as **multiple choice questionnaires**, or perhaps **games**, or the incorporation of **animations** and **simulations**;
- Opportunities for students to receive **feedback** on their work and progress.

Many studies show, especially in the early stages, that the quality of support for learners (online and offline) is highly important for a successful learning experience. Careful course design is not cheap in comparison to more traditional educational development, (particularly as costs are front-loaded) but studies would indicate that it need not be any more expensive in the medium term, and in fact, because of the scalability, might prove to be more cost-effective in the long term. Neither is elearning less of a workload for staff, though human resources might be deployed differently, according to the learning needs of any particular course. In selecting the specific blend in course design it is important to appreciate two key points:

1. The learning situation of the participants: for example, it would be inappropriate to use **videoconferencing** to students if all that is required is to talk to them, or if learners would find it difficult to access such expensive and specialised facilities; **audioconference** facilities might be preferable. Similarly, directing learners to online journals and **digitizing** journal articles for inclusion in the VLE may not be appropriate if elearners lack **bandwidth** (such as **broadband**) and therefore experience difficulties in their ability to **download** the

articles. Perhaps the articles could be recorded on CD and posted to the students.

2. The learning style preference of the learners. We know from experience that people learn best by different means: some people prefer to huddle up with a book; others prefer direct action and still others would choose talking, or video images, to assimilate new information. Obviously there are limitations, both technical and financial, on the provision of the same information in multiple formats, but experiments with **blended learning**, and with **dual mode institutions** would seem to indicate considerable scope for the expansion of this style in the future. The choice of the selected media format should reflect the nature of the learning activity and the type(s) of learning resources that are to be made available to the learner. This may allow for various combinations of media for different learners and learning situations e.g. a powerpoint style presentation on a VLE, with an accompanying **audio** file, may suit one group of learners, while others might prefer to receive the powerpoint slides as an **attachment** to an **email**, with a follow-up telephone call or audioconference discussion.

Selecting a course design that provides **motivation** for the elearner to engage with the learning resources, while not allowing the ICT to dictate the terms of that engagement is tricky, but of fundamental importance. Ideally the technology should fade into the background as learners become more confident in using the **hardware** and **software** applications. Allowing some level of **self-directed learning** and learner control over the pace and style of the way that s/he wants to learn can be a liberating as well as a richly stimulating experience.

COURSEWARE

Any type of instructional or educational course delivered via a **software** program or over the **internet**.

CSCW

Computer Supported Cooperative Work is a generic term that encompasses the enabling systems, services, **hardware** and **software** to support the way people work in groups. The trend toward team work in organisations and toward communication amongst learners in higher education has fuelled the development of these systems. The term CSCW includes the psychological, social and organisational effects of online group work, and the interface to the shared environment is a central feature of CSCW systems. Other important issues are support for group presence, concurrency control and shared information spaces. Some software supports both real-time and **asynchronous** communication, and same place and distributed working.

CYBERLEARNING

This is a synonym for elearning and is not widely used.

CYBERSPACE

This is a term invented to describe the concept of the space where participants can meet **online** to form **communities** on the **internet** to share information, exchange ideas, and generally take part in online discussion (and in the case of elearning, to access course content and resources). The term has science fiction origins, but is now commonly used to explain the notion of a 'virtual place' where online information can be archived and exchanges can take place between individuals. In elearning terms, learners occupy cyberspace when they exchange **email**, join a **chatroom** or other computer mediated communication (**CMC**) and when they take part in learning conversations on **discussion boards** or other managed learning environments (**MLE**).

DATABASE

A type of **software** designed to store and retrieve data in an ordered manner. Most database programs will allow users to search for key themes, re-order data and perhaps allow elementary analysis of the results, e.g. produce graphs or other forms of **graphics**. An advantage of the more complex databases is that they can record multiple character-istics of a sample population and can therefore enable cross-comparison between variables. Connections to **web**-based databases are increasingly being used by commercial retailers to customise the selection of prod-ucts that they can recommend to potential customers, and this technol-ogy has powerful educational potential when linked to resources such as **online libraries** and educational **portals**.

DESKTOP

In computing terms, the desktop is usually the image of the computer screen when the user first switches the computer on, and before any **software** applications are started, or any 'windows' are opened. The desktop is used as a metaphor to refer to an actual desk top where the user can place any files and/or documents that they want to display. Usually the desktop will display a small number of **icons** of the most frequently used documents, files, folders, and software applications that are used on that computer.

DIGITAL DIVIDE

A term used to describe the discrepancy between people who have access to and the resources to use new information and communication tools, such as the **internet**, and people who do not. The term also describes the discrepancy between those who have the skills, knowledge and abilities to use the technologies and those who do not. The digital divide can exist between those living in rural areas and those living in urban areas, between the educated and uneducated, between economic classes, and on a global scale between more and less industrially developed nations.

DIGITIZING

The act of electronically copying printed material into a digital format, usually for dissemination to remote learners via a **VLE** or **MLE**. A common use is for academic papers and/or chapters of text books to be digitized and included as relevant reading material on **distributed education** courses where learners do not have ready access to a large conventional library. Digitized copies of articles may be stored on secure sites that require **password** access, such as an institutional VLE, some **online libraries** or subject-related **portals** that are related to educational purposes. Digitization has the advantage of making high quality resources (including hard-to-get and out-of-print materials) available to a geographically distributed group of learners, but is subject to the usual restrictions on **copyright** and **plagiarism**.

DISCUSSION BOARD

A variation of a **bulletin board system** (BBS) that allows learners and **tutors** to engage in an extended, structured dialogue on topics of relevance to their course of study. Most **VLE** and **MLE** have discussion boards as part of their structural components and they are frequently crucial in establishing the level of group **interaction** that leads to the formation of **online** learning **communities** and **feedback** from both staff and fellow learners. Due to the fundamental importance of discussion boards in stimulating interaction, and due to the importance of this interaction in promoting deeper levels of learning, some tutors allocate marks to students for the quality and quantity of their **postings** to the course discussion board. In this way the discussion board can be used as an educational forum for learners; as an important way of encouraging learners to engage with other sources of learning materials; and also as a means of **assessment** of the level of engagement of the student with the learning process.

DISTRIBUTED EDUCATION

Among the terms that are being used to describe forms of learning in **online** and mixed delivery format, or simply educational delivery that is different from the 'traditional' approach, the concept of distributed learning is increasingly finding favour. Part of the appeal of this concept is that it is vaguely descriptive and so appears to cover a variety of circumstances, while at the same time being specific enough to convey the idea that it is not simply referring to single-location **face-to-face** (**f2f**) delivery. The 'distributed' description applies mainly to a) a form of distance education that is delivered across a wide geographical area, perhaps to multi-site campuses and/or local **learning centres**; and b) a form of **blended learning** in which the teaching and learning resources are distributed across a range of media types and communication styles. The intention of the term is to describe the process rather than a particular theory of learning, and usually refers to a form of educational delivery that is distributed in the context of *both* location and learning resources. In relation to the location of students, blended learning implies that both campus-based students and those who are at remote sites from the **tutor** are able to access the same **modules** and courses, perhaps as part of the same 'class' but certainly over the same time duration. In practice these learners may be scattered across a number of learning centres, partner colleges, or in some cases individual homes or workplaces. There is no rule to differentiate whether they are distributed over three separate sites or 300.

Similarly, the concept of 'distributed resources' conveys an explicit understanding that a wide variety of **courseware**, learning styles, resources, communication tools and types of **assessment** will be employed in the educational provision. A practical example might be of a module on a degree programme that is delivered to students on the same campus as the tutor, but also to thirty or forty other locations. Some of the students may choose to visit another college in the **network,** or drop into a local learning centre for specific study tasks. All of the learners are joined through the same **VLE** and access the course in an **asynchronous** manner over the same semester. Learners at the main campus or subsidiary colleges may choose to borrow books from the library of that institution, while those studying from work or home may place a greater reliance on access to online articles and journals. Some students may prefer to visit local learning centres in order to use restricted **portals** giving access to specialist academic publications that the institution subscribes to, or to use special equipment such as **videoconference** facilities or complex **software** shared over **broadband**. Students on the main campus may elect to meet face-to-face with their course tutor to discuss set topics, while others in more remote locations may prefer to **audioconference**, **videoconference**, or speak to their tutor by **email**, ordinary telephone calls, or through applications such as **instant messaging** and/or **Netmeeting**. Although the greater emphasis on flexibility is generally positive, this needs to be balanced with the added costs of providing very similar educational materials in different formats for perhaps relatively small numbers of students, and this is an important consideration in the **course design** of distributed education.

Web links

QAA Code of practice: Collaborative provision and **flexible** and distributed learning (including elearning) http://www.qaa.ac.uk/academicinfrastructure/codeOfPractice/section2/collab2004.pdf

DOMAIN NAME

Quite simply, this is the common 'address' on the **web** to allow users to locate an individual **webpage**. Web locations will also have a technical, digital numerical, identifier known as the IP address (Internet Protocol) but these tend to be more clumsy and difficult to remember. A typical domain name will combine a unique combination of identification to locate the host **server** computer in an **internet** search. Examples are normally prefixed by www (standing for world wide web) and appear in the form www.uhi.ac.uk or www.bbc.co.uk where 'uhi' stands for University of the Highlands and Islands, and 'bbc' denotes the British Broadcasting Corporation. The suffix 'ac' indicates an academic institution and 'uk' locates the country of registration. Other indicators include 'org' for organisation, and 'com' for company. Usually the root domain name indicates the **homepage** of the organisation, with additional webpages built up by adding extensions to the link, such as http://www.uhi.ac.uk/academicpartners/index.shtm

DOWNLOAD

To transfer data onto a PC from another computer or **network**. This term is often confused with the term **upload**, as the information that a user downloads onto their own computer has frequently been uploaded to the network by another user somewhere else. The speed of the download is governed both by the size and complexity of the data files being transferred, and also by the **bandwidth** available to the user. Generally speaking, small, simple files can be downloaded quite quickly on most modern machines, but larger files, or complex data such as **graphics**, interactive maps, **video clips** and **software** may need higher bandwidth connections (so-called **broadband**) in order to download them with a reasonable speed and accuracy. Slow download times are a source of frustration for many elearners, and it is not uncommon for the computer screen to 'freeze' or disconnect entirely if the **internet** connection is overloaded. For this reason course designers need to be wary in the construction of their **MLE** course sites that no unnecessary graphics or very large text files are included without either giving learners sufficient warning, or giving them the option/choice to download or not. In **distributed education**, some courses may include these large or complex files on a compact disk (CD) in order to overcome the need for students to download large quantities of data over mediocre internet connections.

DROPBOX

A **software** facility of many types of **VLE** or **MLE** that allows elearners to submit their **assessment** materials (usually anonymously) for marking by their course **tutor**. Learners send their piece of work to the dropbox in a manner similar to sending an **email** with an **attachment**, and depending on the sophistication of the VLE or MLE a message will be sent to one marker (or more) and a receipt of acknowledgement will be sent to the learner. Tutors can then recover the submitted pieces of work after the assignment deadline by accessing a special, **password** protected area of the MLE. The dropbox has an advantage over assignments that are simply emailed to tutors in that they can preserve the anonymity of the students until the work has been marked and tutors are ready to give **feedback** to the learners.

DUAL MODE INSTITUTIONS

Universities and other educational institutions that teach on-campus students and also offer full programmes at a distance are often referred to as dual mode institutions. Usually the distance students have the same exams as the on-campus students. Dual mode institutions are prevalent in countries with a federal system of government where states or provinces are responsible for higher education. Examples are Canada, Australia and the US. Some dual mode universities used print-based teaching for the distance students, often with some additional media support such as audio-cassettes or telephone **tutoring**. Others used lectures to remote classrooms delivered by satellite or **videoconference**. Many dual mode institutions are now moving to fully **online** delivery for distance students.

ECDL

European Computer Driving Licence. This is an internationally recognised qualification in computer competency covering various aspects such as basic file-management, word-processing, spreadsheets, **database** management, **email** and **web** and presentations. The certificate based upon relating practical applications to theory is designed as a benchmark qualification for computer users, especially those with a need to demonstrate their competence for the advancement of their career.

Web links

http://www.ecdl.co.uk

EDUTAINMENT

This is a compound word, bringing together 'education' and 'entertainment'. It specifically refers to programmes or activities that use forms of mass entertainment to introduce opportunities for public education in a non-formal manner. Although its use has a relatively long history on radio (e.g. 'The Archers') and on television (e.g. 'Blue Peter' and 'Sesame Street') each of which have been successfully used to incorporate educational messages and activities for the mass audience, there has been a very slow uptake in formal higher education. The rapid growth of digital **games** as a hobby and the continuing spread of elearning has encouraged some educators to combine elements of the two in order to stimulate greater **interaction** with learning materials, particularly among young learners. The incorporation of elements such as quizzes on the **VLE** or **MLE** to provide self-test opportunities and/or formative **assessment** and to give quick **feedback** to learners has resulted in a number of educational games that include, for instance, **multiple choice questions** (**MCQ**). The concept has much in common with 'infotainment' a portmanteau term that combines 'information' and 'entertainment' in a manner that seeks to make news and current affairs items appear entertaining to a wider demographical market sector. Both terms seek to reach out in an informal manner to new client groups that traditional forms of education (or news coverage) have failed to engage with and/or who are apparently less able to take advantage of more traditional learning methods. Edutainment is of course not restricted to **online** varieties and it has been possible to combine educational games (e.g. business games) with other learning resources to utilise the social learning aspect of the games in a form of **distributed education**.

ELECTRONIC FORUM

A term largely used in the US referring to a **discussion board** or, in some contexts, the process of **computer conferencing**.

EMAIL

Messages are usually text sent from one person to another via computer. Email can also be sent automatically to a large number of addresses. In elearning, email has several uses: one-to-one communication between, say, student and **tutor**, and one-to-many communication from, say, the tutor to all the students in the group. Most **VLEs** have a separate email facility for messages that are personal or not relevant to the whole group.

EMOTICONS

The reliance of **email** and other forms of **CMC** on the written word is often thought to cause a very concise, even terse dialogue between users, which is frequently misinterpreted as brusqueness or rudeness. Occasionally these comments may lead to **flaming** or flame wars requiring time and patience to resolve. As a consequence of this, some users include emoticons in their text (shorthand for 'emotional **icons**') to indicate the spirit in which their message is sent. Examples might include the familiar smiley face :o) to indicate a joking remark and corresponding variations for sadness :o(or for confusion :o/ and so on. Some newer applications such as **instant messaging** software may include a range of customised emoticons to encourage non-verbal cues to be included within **text messages**.

EPORTFOLIO

Electronic portfolios (also referred to as eportfolios or webfolios) are increasingly recognised as a valuable tool not only for learners but also for instructors and academic organisations. Eportfolio implementation is a major development area in elearning. Three categories of use can be distinguished, though the boundaries are not clear-cut. Eportfolios are used:

* for **assessment**;
* as a form of personal development planning for staff and students;
* as a tool to support reflection on learning and teaching.

The growth of eportfolios is fuelled by a number of broad factors: the dynamics of functioning in a knowledge economy, the changing nature of learning, and the changing needs of the learner. One way of describing them might be, 'a dynamic, ever-growing, annotated CV'.

An 'idealised' scenario for the use of an eportfolio by a student would be: the student enters each item as a unique object with **metadata** to enable easy access; the items can be grouped and permissions granted for different audiences. For assessment purposes, the learner draws items from the bank of items and sends a link to the instructor; for employment purposes, the learner chooses items which show a required skill.

One of the anticipated benefits of eportfolios is that they should facilitate the process of learners being able to make connections between learning experiences, especially between formal and informal experiences. They should also provide the metacognitive elements learners require to plan future learning needs based on their previous successes and failures.

Eportfolios, as opposed to portfolios, are still in the expansion and experiment phase of development. However, it is possible to summarise current uses for students as follows:

- The eportfolio is embedded into the curriculum as a tool to support learning;
- There is a strong emphasis on supporting reflection on learning;
- There is an intention to encourage students to take responsibility for their own learning.

However, persuading students of the potential benefits and of the need to take seriously the business of continually updating their portfolio is something of an uphill struggle. Some universities are now offering credit for the recording and reflection aspects of eportfolio development.

For academic staff, eportfolio updating may well be mandatory and related to promotion and salary increases. An academic eportfolio might consist of a résumé, a statement of teaching philosophy, examples of teaching practice (such as **course design, feedback** from students or extracts from **interactions** with students) and reflective processes which demonstrate professional growth.

Many universities that have embedded eportfolios into the curriculum have done so in a way that enables assessment for learning by means of inbuilt, **online**, instantaneous feedback systems. Assessment which consists of the student selecting pieces of work and providing a linking overview, is a more common use of the portfolio concept. Another aspect of assessment is self-assessment and this practice is strongly associated with the introduction of eportfolios. For example, students might be asked to reflect on their learning, and to diagnose their strengths and weaknesses. This regular reflection process then forms part of their eportfolio. Students might also be expected to identify two or three skills or areas of study they would like to develop, and accompanying this would be their plan of action for accomplishing this development. In short, an eportfolio in an educational context, consists of an archive of past work, evidence of current activities, assessment and reflection, plus plans for the future. It is apparent that students need advice and support from **tutors** and mentors to carry out this level of **self-directed learning**.

The process of creating an eportfolio consists of collecting pieces of work, assessments, presentations, websites, blogs etc., explaining how the learning experiences relate to course content or learning objectives and documenting this with evidence from the pieces submitted. Students can share their eportfolio with staff and/or other students, who can add their comments.

While new 'purpose-built' eportfolio **software** is available commercially, many users have built systems using existing software, such as **HTML** editors – Dreamweaver or FrontPage, Web Design tools such as Flash and Authorware, blogs and **Wikis**, and finally Content Management Systems. One of the areas of eportfolio development is the integration of **blogging** and eportfolio **software**, thus underlining the aim of eportfolios to support reflection and self-directed learning.

Web links

http://webcenter1.aahe.org/electronicportfolios/index.html
http://www.e-learningcentre.co.uk/eclipse/Resources/
eportfolios.htm
http://www.eradc.org/index.php

Further reading

Cambridge, Barbara L. (1996). The paradigm shifts: examining quality of teaching through assessment of student learning. *Innovative Higher Education*, 20(4), 287–297.

Cambridge, a noted expert on portfolios, suggests that student learning is enhanced when faculty develop course portfolios to document their own learning in a course and then share the portfolio with students.

EXPERIENTIAL LEARNING

A theory of adult education and **lifelong learning** that suggests learners acquire knowledge and skills in a more profound manner when they actually are engaged with the subject matter, rather than considering it at a distance or in an abstract form. The emphasis upon individuals having a direct experience of the learning materials means that experiential learning is not restricted to the formal education system, and indeed some educationalists have argued that in its most pure form, the learning experiences should directly relate to events in the life of the individual learner. The ability for elearners to have heightened **interaction** with other learners (both globally and over time) using electronic means such as **email**, a **VLE**, and/or other forms of **distributed education**, suggests that there are rich opportunities to share experiences with other elearners in an informal but structured way. In this process, learners can share experiences, reflect upon the discussions in the light of their own experience, form and test concepts or ideas in a concrete manner (e.g. by carrying out a subsequent activity) and then observe and reflect upon their new experiences arising from that activity. The process is therefore circular and potentially endless, frequently summarised by Kolb's learning cycle, although this theory is not without its critics.

Web links

http://www.infed.org/biblio/b-explrn.htm
http://reviewing.co.uk/research/experiential.learning.htm

FACE-TO-FACE (f2f)

With the evolution of **distributed education** and a wide variety of different ways to make contact between individuals and groups who are geographically dispersed, the term face-to-face, or simply f2f, has come to refer to meetings that take place in person, i.e. with the participants in the same room. Increasingly in distributed education it has become necessary to specify a 'f2f meeting' in order to differentiate from the more common areas of educational **interactivity** such as by **video-conference**, by **audioconference**, or through a variety of **computer mediated conference** styles such as **virtual seminars**, shorter **instant messaging** connections, or communication via **software** such as **Netmeeting** or **Skype**.

FACILITATOR

This is the term used for the **online** tutor who guides and organises discussion. The online environment is much less teacher-centric than the **face-to-face** (**f2f**) classroom and the use of 'facilitator' rather than teacher reflects this change in role and power.

FAQs

Frequently Asked Question files are **online** informational lists in question and answer format of common enquiries from users. They include standard responses prepared either by the instructor or technical assistant. The aim is to assist new users and to avoid repetitive offline enquiries. They are often built up through successive presentations of a course.

FEEDBACK

This is a general term used to describe any structured comments, written or verbal, that are given to learners on work that they have submitted for **assessment**. Experience has shown that carefully considered comments from the **tutor** to the learner on the work being assessed are much more effective in the learning process when they closely follow the submission and marking of the assignment. Most universities have a regulation that states the maximum period allowed for some form of formal feedback on the submitted work of the learner, normally two to three weeks. The transmission of feedback is crucial in helping the learner gain an awareness and appreciation of their strong/weak points, and the reasons for the grade of mark that they have obtained. Timely and appropriate feedback is especially important in distance education as this may be the only real contact that a learner has with their tutor, and hence the only significant opportunity to learn constructively from any mistakes. In terms of elearning, feedback is also a critical component of the learner-tutor **interaction**. When dealing with learners who are studying at locations remote from the main location of the tutor, these are effectively distance students and have a similar dependence on the speed and quality of tutor feedback as a measure of their progress. This is true even when the learner is participating in **distributed education** and elearning (text-based **online** feedback is only one of the conduits of communication with tutorial staff and other learners. In the situation where elearning is a key component of learning for campus-based students, feedback is no less important, but of course may be provided by a variety of means, including written comments, **face-to-face** (**f2f**) tutorials and/or seminars.

Feedback frequently follows an unwritten rule that the comments by the tutor should begin by praising some aspect of the submitted work, followed by carefully worded comments identifying the main aspects that could be improved to obtain a higher mark, and finishing by making some positive suggestions as to how the learner could build on this to improve future performance. The scope of the feedback can be very narrow, or very wide ranging according to the subject, the level, and usually covers such items as developing an argument, proper referencing, developing critical thinking, providing evidence for assertions, deepening knowledge, and generally improving the communication skills of the learner. As with other aspects of elearning, feedback to students provided electronically by **email** or through a subject **discussion board**, can frequently be used to dramatic effect due to the speed and immediacy of the media. The introduction of new technological applications such as **instant messaging**, and connections by **Skype** and/or **videoconference** into elearning practice offer opportunities for more or less immediate feedback to learners even if they are widely scattered geographically.

In practice there is no difference between feedback that is given for formative assessments and that which is given for a summative assessment and final grade, but there may be a great deal of difference to the way these are treated by the educational establishment, and correspondingly on their impact on the learner. Feedback on formative assessments allows the learner to build up a good picture of how well they are performing, and what areas require improving before the submission of the final summative assessment so critical for the final grade. On the other hand, providing feedback only on the summative assessment means that a learner does not have the opportunity to improve on subsequent assessment. For this reason some educators have developed the practice of providing 'concurrent feedback' intermittently during assessments, and again this style has translated very effectively to elearning in general. (It is easy for students to submit drafts to the tutor to check that they are on the right track.) Key factors in providing good feedback are:

- It should compare the performance of the learner with some other performance of an appropriate (good) standard;
- It provides guidance and cites evidence for the tutor's comments;
- It is presented to the learner in a timely manner;

- The advice is useable and clearly explained;
- It presents suggestions, and perhaps further reading, to allow the learner to improve on their performance;
- It clearly relates the learners performance to the grade acquired.

In some instances and at some levels of undergraduate studies, feedback can be given immediately to elearners by the use of online **multiple-choice questionnaires (MCQ)** that have been written to give an automatic response. In these cases the selection of a wrong answer will not only indicate the error immediately to the learner, but will explain why this selection is incorrect. The choice of a correct answer will also provide some further detail, and will allow the learner to proceed to the next question, providing an overall grade at the end if required. Some educationalists dislike MCQ as an assessment option, claiming that it promotes superficial as opposed to deep learning, but in elearning they have frequently been included as short in-text tests of student understanding of topics on the **MLE**, to provide some formative self-assessment and quick, constructive feedback.

FILE TRANSFER PROTOCOL (FTP)

A computer agreement protocol that enables entire files to be transferred between one computer and another over the **internet**.

FIREWALL

A firewall is a piece of **software** and/or **hardware** used to provide security within and between computer **networks**. In general a firewall provides network security to users **online** and defines the zone of **trust** that exists within **communities**, from the open access free-for-all of the **internet**, to the relatively safe environment of an organisational **intranet**. A firewall filters out unwelcoming and hostile communications and prevents other networks gaining access to a private network if they do not have the necessary permissions.

FLAMING (OR FLAME WAR)

An exchange of intemperate, hostile, or abusive messages via electronic media, such as **discussion boards**, by **instant messaging**, or by group

email. The immediacy of these media, together with the tendency for them to be text-based and relatively short, has given rise to a tendency for users to respond quickly to previous messages. In some cases the brevity of the response, coupled with the lack of detailed ways to convey emotion, can produce seemingly strong feelings which can escalate quickly into heated **online** exchanges, or flame wars. New elearners, especially, are encouraged to pause for thought before replying to provocative messages, and more frequent users often resort to **emoticons** to give the suggestion of their humour in the context of the message. Flaming is the online equivalent to an explosive outburst in a **face-to-face** (**f2f**) meeting, and while this may sometimes provoke a useful exchange of radically different opinions, its continued use is not to be recommended or tolerated by the responsible **moderator**.

FLEXIBLE LEARNING

This term is used most commonly in Australia, though not exclusively there. Flexible learning is very close in meaning to '**open learning**' as both are focused on the ability for learners to decide what, where, when and how they learn. Elearning is considered to be a component of flexible learning or possibly one type of flexible learning. In Australia the term is used in relation to both vocational programmes and higher education, whereas in the UK, it is primarily used in reference to further rather than higher education.

A **student-centred** approach to education underpins the concept of flexible learning. The following characteristics of flexible learning indicate a strong similarity with distance education and elearning. For example:

- Flexible learning relies less on **face-to-face** (**f2f**) teaching and more on guided independent learning; teachers become **facilitators** of the learning process directing students to appropriate resources, tasks and learning outcomes;
- Flexible learning places greater reliance on high quality learning resources using a range of technologies (e.g., print, CD-ROM, video, audio, the **internet**);
- Flexible learning provides opportunities to communicate outside traditional teaching times;
- Flexible learning makes use of information and communications technology (**ICT**) and multi-skilled teams to produce, deliver, teach and administer the courses.

As with elearning, IT is often central to much of the implementation of flexible learning, for example in delivering learning resources, providing a communications facility, administering units and student **assessment**, and hosting student support systems. Related to this is the use of teams rather than individual academics undertaking all stages of unit planning, development, delivery, assessment and maintenance. Instead, other professionals are often required to provide specific skills, for example in **instructional design**, desktop publishing, **web** development and administration and maintenance of programmes.

As with open learning, flexible learning is an aspiration or aim, rather than a method of education. The aspiration is to provide access and equity; in other words, to reduce or eliminate any barriers that stand between the learner and the learning environment. Examples of barriers are: previous qualifications, geographical location, lifestyle and ability to pay. It is rare to find an accredited programme that removes all barriers. Totally flexible learning would include:

- open entry with no prerequisite qualifications required;
- multiple annual start dates;
- both time and location of study determined by the student;
- the pace of progress through the course determined by the student;
- assessment and content of the course negotiated by the student;
- no cost to the student for studying the course.

It is questionable whether any such program, if it did exist, would have enough structure, dynamism and challenge to be successful. In short, some flexibility is good, but more is not necessarily better.

Three educational principles are evident in most programmes that aim to be flexible: opportunities to learn by doing, opportunities to contextualise learning and individual **feedback** to learners on their work. Of course these principles are not unique to flexible learning; arguably they should underpin all forms of teaching and learning.

Learning by doing is particularly relevant for vocational programmes, but is appropriate at all educational levels. Even textbooks and other print material should contain tasks and activities with answers preferably at the back. Although print is a more flexible medium, computer-based materials can be more motivating, interactive and dynamic than print.

Flexible learning should offer students the opportunity to tailor some or all of the learning content, process, outcomes or assessment to their individual circumstances. For example, assessment could allow students to apply the topic to their employment or desired employment. The content of the course could offer students the possibility of studying in depth the aspects of the subject that most interest them.

The benefit to learners of detailed, sympathetic and timely feedback on submitted work cannot be over-estimated. Students who return to formal education after some time, usually need reassurance, praise for what is good in their work, and careful but honest feedback on what needs to be improved. Most important is specific advice on how to improve.

An aspect of flexibility that is highly valued by non-traditional students is the facility for recognition of prior learning. This allows students to prepare a case demonstrating what they have learned from employment or other experience and submit this for consideration for partial credit towards a degree. Related to this facility is the possibility of transferring credits gained from one institution to another. Because of employment moves, family and various kinds of personal crises, the need for students to gain their degree from a number of institutions is a growing phenomenon.

As with distance education and elearning, flexible delivery requires more planning before the course begins. The course designers need to consider developing or providing a range of additional material to the core content of the course. Background material might be necessary, as students will not all have the same starting knowledge. Remedial material might also be needed for students lacking particular skills. Finally, experienced course designers know how important clarity is in all instructions and assessment questions. When opportunities for face-to-face clarification are few, it is essential to prevent confusion by careful presentation in the first place. One way of doing this is to pilot materials with potential or actual students. Through feedback or observation, course designers can build up their expertise in how to write clearly and in what kinds of problems students have with course content.

Flexible delivery of education has two components: enhancing the educational experience for learners and widening participation in education to those normally excluded.

Web links

http://ncode.uow.edu.au/
http://www.city.londonmet.ac.uk/deliberations/flex.learning/

GAMES AND GAMING

The popularity of **online** games and collaborative games that are played over the **internet**, has encouraged some educationalists to experiment with educational games as a resource in elearning. These games can range from very simple question-and-answer type (some of these constructed to resemble popular television game shows) to very sophisticated **virtual reality** constructions that allow learners to engage in **role play**. The essence of games in elearning is that they help to make learning fun, and learners can acquire knowledge and skills in the process, sometimes almost without realising it. In this respect gaming can be regarded as a form of **experiential learning**, or **activity-based learning**, in which the learners gain knowledge by doing an activity, rather than from simply thinking about it in more abstract terms. This can be conducted individually or in **groupwork**. Games have been used in elearning at almost all educational levels, from primary schools through higher education, but it has been argued that their main attraction is for younger participants. Games can be used to provide **simulations** of educational activities that are prohibitively expensive or too dangerous for learners to try in real life, such as the design, construction and furnishing of a building, or the experimental handling of radioactive or caustic substances.

GIF

This stands for Graphics Interchange Format and refers to a specific type of computer file used especially with **webpages** for transferring **graphics** easily between computers and across **networks**. A GIF file is compressed to reduce the size of the file without losing any visual accuracy, but the restriction to 256 colours means that they are better for diagrams and simple **web** images, but are not usually used to transfer photographs (see **jpeg**).

GLOBAL EDUCATION

There are a number of aspects to the concept of global education depending on whether the focus is on the content of education or the provision of education.

In terms of the content of higher education, globalisation means the process of integrating an international, intercultural, or global dimension into the purpose, functions or delivery of education. For example, it includes the tailoring of an offering to include clear, grammatically correct text that eliminates slang, gender references, and cultural or generational idioms. It can also mean the use of **case studies** and examples from outside national borders, and the introduction of content about the interconnectedness of systems – cultural, ecological, economic, political and technological. In fact, globalisation is as much a way of thinking as it is a science, and is leading to increased cross-disciplinary focus in all subjects.

In terms of provision, the driving force is the increasing demand for education worldwide, but especially from developing countries. Regulatory and policy frameworks of universities reflect national priorities and concerns. Cross border activity tends to undermine these policies. However, in an increasingly international environment in which both markets and professions have become global, the national character of policy frameworks creates more and more tensions. Institutions already acknowledge this and are developing partnerships, consortia and **networks** to strengthen their position in the global arena. Universities from North America, Europe and Australia have taken initiatives to extend their educational provision to this international higher education market, by active recruitment of international, fee-paying students to the home institution, by establishing branch campuses or franchising and twinning agreements with local institutions, or via distance education and elearning and other transnational activities. The international demand for higher education has also invited new providers from outside the higher education sector to enter the scene.

The transition to a knowledge society has created another global imperative: scientific research and development of technologies are crucial activities in a knowledge and information driven society and will become even more important in the future. Not only in the core countries of the developed world, but increasingly also in other parts of the globe, research and development activities have become the driver of economic growth and social development. Competition for research grants and for large contracts between universities and companies, and trade in academic personnel especially in scientific fields have led to a highly competitive, global academic market place. Global education clearly presents new opportunities, challenges and risks.

Further reading

Burbules, N. C. and Torres, C. A. (2000). *Globalization and Education: Critical Perspectives*, London: Routledge. The introduction is available on the **web**: http://faculty.ed.uiuc.edu/burbules/ncb/papers/global.html

GRAPHICS

Any image, diagram, or illustration that is reproduced in digital format and used to elaborate a **webpage** or another computer file can be considered a graphic. Graphics can be used as simple decoration and/or can function as **hyperlinks** to navigate to another **internet** location. Due to the complexity of the data stored, graphics can take up a large amount of computer memory, and will also take a long time to **download** for a user with a low **bandwidth** connection to the **internet**. For this reason, graphics should be used carefully, whether on a webpage or embedded in another document, such as a word-processed file. Frustration in attempting to view or download large graphics files is a frequent cause of elearner dissatisfaction with **online** resources, and it is good design practice to indicate such large files by bringing them to the attention of the learner (e.g. 'the graphic at this link is 7KB') and either open them on a different webpage window, or as an **attachment** such as a **jpeg** file.

GROUPWORK

Many educators regard this as one of the mainstays of **online** courses. Group assignments and meetings can be facilitated by **email**, private **chatrooms, bulletin boards** and voice calls. There are pitfalls however to the use of groupwork: many people are antagonistic and resent others in the group who do not 'pull their weight'; different learning styles and study patterns can make the work difficult to coordinate, and group marks can be contentious. Solutions include: building more measures that support positive interdependence, individual accountability, and collaborative skills; increasing opportunities for the socio-emotional and affective exchanges between learners; adjusting the **tutor's** and the learners' role for CSCL environments; and increasing social presence, i.e. reducing the perceived distance between learners.

See also: **collaborative work/learning**.

HACKER

Although this term began simply as a description of someone who is a serious computer programmer, it has evolved to mean a person who uses their programming expertise to 'break through' the security system of computer **networks**. A typical hacker might violate the **firewall** of a **password** protected network in order to gain access to confidential data and/or to advertise the fact that they have been clever enough to break through the organisation's security. A hacker is not the same as a person who creates a **virus** with the deliberate aim of causing damage, and many hackers would now consider themselves to be fighting for the free use of the **internet** against those corporate interests that would like to restrict and control access for commercial benefits.

HARDWARE

This is the physical components of a computing system or **network** e.g. the computer processing unit itself, together with the screen (or VDU) and any other peripheral devices such as a printer, **modem**, audio speakers, **webcam**, external CD drive, cables etc. Hardware is normally the host or the means for **software** to function, that is to say software gives the instructions for the hardware to carry out certain tasks, such as printing or displaying information from an **internet** connection.

HELPLINE/HELPDESK

As increasing numbers of learners seek access to educational material in an **online** format, and from geographically scattered locations (see **distributed education**) there has been a realisation that some technical assistance is often necessary. A helpdesk usually provides telephone advice from **network** experts, often including an 'out of hours' or 24/7 service to cover generic questions on problems that learners encounter. Typical problems would include learners that have forgotten their **password**, or have difficulty in connecting to the institutional **VLE** or **MLE**, or perhaps have a difficulty in navigating the VLE to locate the **discussion board** or other component relevant to their studies. The value of the helpdesk is that it uses simple, immediate technology (e.g. a telephone) to connect people who have a problem, *when* they have the problem, to a specialist who can log their call and either provide an immediate answer, or else connect to a relevant specialist who will make contact. Although it seems that many of the helpdesk enquiries are relatively trivial, there is a great comfort factor for novice elearners in knowing that help is only a phone call away.

HOAX EMAIL

A mildly malicious or criminal **email** message that is intended to cause mischief. Examples would include the regular **spam** email that promises the reader a share in a small fortune in return for some assistance (a confidence trick) or the circular email that warns of a non-existent **virus** and encourages the reader to pass the message to all the friends with whom s/he is in email contact (a spoof). Hoax email does not generally damage an individual computer **network** (except when millions of message are sent and the **server** is overloaded to the point of collapse) but the cumulative cost of handling them, and the nuisance value to users of identifying and deleting them from the system is estimated at many millions of pounds per year.

HOMEPAGE

This is the opening page of a series of pages on the **web**. The homepage usually is the reference location of the **web presence** of an individual or organisation and is identified by a **URL**. Normally the homepage will contain a number of **hyperlinks** to other **webpages** and is used as a 'shop window' to display other resources that the owners of the webpage want to draw to the attention of the user. The homepage can be considered the root page of a complex website and users can navigate their way through a large variety of other web-based resources by using the homepage as a navigational point, usually by clicking on a button labelled 'home' to return to the opening page.

HTML

Hyper Text Markup Language is a language used to create a **webpage** that allows text, **graphics** and other information to be viewed through a **browser**. At its simplest this consists of a series of commands that are used to identify headings, font sizes, colours, and links to other sites that are incorporated into the design of the webpage. In conventional use, most users will not see these commands, as they remain hidden in the final screen presentation. Users can view the HTML structure of a specific webpage by going to that page then selecting <view> then <source> from the **toolbar** at the top of the screen. Initially HTML was presented in a very loose structure that was interpreted by the web

browser, but increasingly strict rules of construction have been applied to govern the language and control more accurately what the **web** designer wishes to express. Some early examples of elearning courses were simply word documents that were converted into HTML and displayed for open access on the **web**. With increasing sophistication, these early attempts were replaced by customised elearning **platforms** and **VLEs**, which gave greater control over the structure and content of the site, but restricted access to authorised users with an institutional **password**. There is a move towards XHTML (Extensible Hyper Text Markup Language) that is similar in structure but with a stricter syntax that will allow for a flexible use of common standards across the various machine readable communications systems using the **internet**.

The first few lines of HTML for the site www.uhi.ac.uk are as follows,

```
<html>
<head>
<title>Welcome to UHI Millennium Institute – &quot;Creat-
ing the University of the Highlands &amp; Islands&quot;
</title>
<meta http-equiv="Content-Type"content="text/html;
charset=iso-8859–1">
<script language="JavaScript1.2"src="includes/browsercheck.js">
</script>
```

HTTP

Hypertext Transfer Protocol was designed to allow publication of materials on the World Wide **Web**. This is a method of request and response for communicating information across the **internet** in a stand-ard manner that allows users to send documents and other digital infor-mation between computers. It follows a standard set of rules for data identification, **authentication** and error correction, and uses **hyper-text** as a means of cross-referencing documents to allow users to access layers of different information from different sources upon request. These documents can be held on a computer anywhere in the world that acts as a **server** to supply documents as **wepages** to users over the internet.

HYPERLINK/HYPERTEXT

A line of text, a **graphic**, or an **icon** on a **webpage** that provides a link to another webpage or **web** based resource when the user clicks on it with the computer mouse. Hyperlinks (whether they are text or images) are constructed using hypertext markup language (**HTML**) that enables identification and visual display when used with a **browser** to navigate a path through the resources on the **internet**. Commonly hypertext is displayed on a webpage in a different colour from the main text and is underlined and/or in bold. Moving the mouse cursor over a hyperlink usually causes the cursor to change from an arrow to a hand with a pointing finger to indicate a link to another 'layer' of resources.

ICON

An image that stands as a symbol and is used in computing to indicate an activity or a location to the user of a particular piece of **software**. An example might be a picture of a folder to indicate a location in which to store files; a representation of a filing cabinet to indicate a location to store electronic folders or documents; or a picture of a printer to indicate the command button to print a current document. Common icons are usually displayed in the **toolbar** of a software application, or on the **desktop** of the user's computer.

ICQ

An early type of **software** for conducting **instant messaging** over the **internet**. It stands for 'I seek you' and has since lost predominance as the only such application due to the wide variety of other commercial instant messaging services that have emerged in recent years.

ICT

Used as a common abbreviation for Information and Communications Technology. This is a very broad descriptive term for any **hardware** or **software**, or even any activity that is related to the use of computers for the generation, storage, transmission and retrieval of information in an electronic format. Early forms of the concept often referred simply to 'information technology' (IT) but the additional component of rapid digital transfer of information between computers in a **network**, and using computers to communicate by **email**, or **videoconferencing** on the **desktop**, over the **internet**, has substantially enlarged the generic use of the term. A significant distinction to emerge in recent years is that, as **software** and the **MLE** for elearning has become more sophisticated and 'user-friendly', learners no longer need to be highly skilled computer programmers in order to use elearning tools and benefit from the educational experience. This has been summed up in the belief that ICT should *support* learners to do the activities that they choose, rather than be the driving factor that *leads* learners to follow the demands of the hardware and software. There is an implicit assumption that a good use of ICT, combined with good elearning **course design**, will encourage the learner to engage with the learning resources and activities rather than with the ICT.

INFORMATION LITERACY

The ability to locate, evaluate, use and communicate information whether textual or visual. This term implies a fusing or integration of library literacy, computer literacy, media literacy, technological literacy, ethics, critical thinking and communication skills. It is a skill fundamental to elearning and can be practiced in **online** courses through activities in which the student is required to search for a particular article, or select the most appropriate article from a **database**, write summaries of papers highlighting key points, explain the essential components of an argument to other students, or evaluate a selection of websites.

INSTANT MESSAGING

A form of electronic messaging similar to **email** but differing in that the communication takes place as a **synchronous** exchange i.e. in real time. Many **internet service providers** (**ISP**) now offer an instant messaging service that allows users of the **network** to identify when colleagues are **online**, enabling them to send and receive short messages immediately. Increasing **convergence** is now encouraging some instant messaging providers to combine with other applications to send **video clips** and **VoIP** as well as conventional **text messages**. The immediacy of instant messaging has encouraged its use in **distributed education** solutions as a useful way of contact between **tutors** and students who are remote from the teaching campus. Typically if a student is on the **web** and is working through some course material but has a problem or question s/he will notice from a screen **icon** whether the tutor (or a fellow student on their course) is also **online**, and can send a short message asking for clarification/explanation. The message is received almost immediately and may result in a quick reply. In supporting online learners, instant messaging usually results in short bursts of text dialogue between two or three individuals in relation to a specific issue, and is therefore a useful means of providing academic guidance when and where it is most needed. Its limitations are that it is restricted to synchronous communications and that it is best for short, concentrated bursts of specific dialogue, in contrast to the depth of reflectivity that is afforded by email and thematic **discussion boards**.

INSTRUCTIONAL DESIGN

A phrase used mainly in the US referring to **course design**.

INTERACTION

Typologies and definitions of **online** interaction have been the subject of much elearning research. Some of the literature distinguishes between interaction with the computer and interaction with other people through the computer. Some research restricts the term interaction to communication with other learners, whereas other research identifies many ways of interacting online: with the interface, with the content, with the **tutor** and with other students. Where interaction is seen as a complex interplay of many kinds of online activity, the key components are: **course design**, learner engagement, tutor inputs and **platform** capabilities. Many elearning researchers have concluded that social interactions play a major part in increasing the total interaction of an online course, and can enhance and further learning.

There is little doubt amongst researchers that the quality of online interaction is an important element in successful elearning. A number of studies have correlated student satisfaction and achievement with interaction levels. Others have shown that students' perceived learning in online courses was related to the level of interaction with the tutor and amongst the students. Furthermore, the quantity of interaction on elearning courses has been shown to be much higher than in **face-to-face** (**f2f**) courses. The quality and usefulness of online interactions, however, are the crucial elements, not the quantity.

At its best, online interaction is knowledge building: students explore issues, examine one another's arguments, agree, disagree and question positions. This kind of interaction contributes to higher order learning through cognitive restructuring or conflict resolution. New ways of understanding the material emerge as a result of contact with different perspectives. Interaction with course content and resource material can also have similar effects. A simple interaction might be an online search to find learning materials or a spreadsheet calculation to solve a problem. A more complex interaction might be a **simulation** or **role play** that enables the learner to explore a problem or **case study** and come to a solution in a non directed manner. Whether the interaction is with other learners or with content, what makes the difference to the learning outcome is the level of the learner's engagement with the ideas.

A number of researchers have demonstrated that social interaction fosters instructional interaction. Students need to feel comfortable about interacting with their peers, and social exchanges are perceived as safer than discussions about course ideas as the group begins the process of getting to know each other. For this reason, most course designers set up areas for social interaction and include activities particularly at the beginning of the course to build social presence and **community**.

Related to social interaction is the expression of emotion, feelings and mood. Novices to the online environment expect interaction to be cold and dry. In fact the opposite is usually the case. Elearning groups often contain exchanges that are warm, close and welcoming.

One of the difficulties with online interaction that sometimes arises in elearning contexts is that all of the messages are excessively polite. This does not create a stimulating learning environment. The tutor needs to step in and model appropriate processes of questioning and challenging.

The following ways of encouraging online interaction are commonly cited:

1. Timely and personal **feedback** from the tutor to learner contributions and questions.
2. Course design which involves highly interactive activities that are designed to encourage, support and even require interaction.
3. Allocating students to small groups of about six or seven to carry out activities and engage in discussion.
4. Course design which includes combinations of voluntary and required responses, and both initiation of and response to messages.
5. Collaborative activities which require collaborations within and among groups.
6. Reinforcement by the tutor of the positive aspects of students' work, which has been shown to lead to improved interaction and subsequently to improved learning.

While some online tutors are concerned to increase interaction, others are overwhelmed by it, especially when students continue to see the tutor as the 'font of all knowledge'. Techniques commonly cited for tutors to manage online interaction are:

1. Encouraging students to put their queries into the **discussion board** area and not to send **email** unless the communication is very personal.
2. Reducing the level of commenting as the course proceeds, focusing on introducing and summarising discussions.
3. Designing activities in which students take on the role of online **moderator** for short periods.
4. Making clear what the tutorial commitment is, including **logging on** times and frequency.

A few researchers have studied the nature of elearning interactions and findings across a range of contexts show a surprising degree of consensus. In the majority of messages, students share information and express a point of view. Between 10 and 30 per cent of messages contain expressions of feeling, such as jokes, compliments and self-disclosures. Very few messages contain questions.

Most elearning environments rely on **asynchronous** interaction as the primary means of communication. However technologies for **synchronous** interaction are developing very quickly and are the focus of experimentation in a number of elearning programs. Text chat has been available for some time, but multiway audio and video are now available on the **desktop**. Some of the uses for synchronous interaction include: decision-making in the process of collaborative activities, contacting the tutor during office hours, and self-help sessions amongst learners. Audio interaction frees learners from typing, and allows them to focus on listening, thinking, speaking and questioning. As an occasional supplement to asynchronous interaction, real-time communication provides immediacy and social presence. Students often report that it improves their **motivation** to study.

It is possible to conclude from research into online interaction that the more comfortable students are with the elearning environment, the more likely they are to interact. Complimenting and acknowledging, and expressing appreciation by both students and tutors are interactive communications that work well in a text-based medium. Tutors and course designers know that when students are interacting well online, the content of the course has been increased in a way that they never could create by other means.

Web links

http://www.sloan-c.org/publications/jaln/v8n4/v8n4_roblyer.asp
http://www.irrodl.org/content/v4.1/fahy.html
http://cade.icaap.org/vol14.2/rourke_et_al.html

INTERNET

The complex, and rapidly extending, network of interlinked computer **networks** is called the internet. Agreement on a common set of protocols enables computers anywhere in the network to communicate with any other computer in the network, using a wide variety of different paths. Schematically, local area networks (**LAN**) for an organisation or a geographical area are joined together in increasingly larger networks, to give a global coverage. This allows common tasks to be performed throughout the network, such as sending/receiving **email**, or **surfing** the **web** for information (e.g. text or **graphics**) contained in **databases**. The internet enables individuals or organisations to connect web **servers** that host information resources and make these resources available to appropriate users on request. The structure of the internet allows for secure areas that require a **password** to enter (often requiring payment), and also areas where information is freely available to all. For this reason, the internet is both a wonderful source of detailed information and source of misinformation or trivia. Learners (formal and non-formal) using the internet require to be critically aware of their sources of information and the possibilities for bias and deception. Although there are an increasing number of reliable resources such as peer-reviewed journals (see **URL** below) and creditable websites provided by international organisations such as the UN, there is also almost limitless scope for lobbyists, advertising and organisational propaganda. It is crucial that (especially new) learners learn early to distinguish between credible information on the internet and those **webpages** from unverifiable sources. The internet is able to support a variety of digital devices other than computers, and consequently provides the central structure for **distributed education** that allows internet connectivity for **videoconferencing**, for **voice-over-internet** (VoIP) telephone conversations, and a variety of **software** applications such as geographical positioning systems or **virtual reality** experiences.

INTERNET CAFÉ

This is a term that has emerged as a generic description of any 'drop in' facility that provides **internet** access for casual users. Normally a private sector operation, it can also be operated through a local library, tourist bureau etc. but normally charges for use and frequently combines **ICT** access with other commercial activities, such as a bookshop, tourist information, or, as the name suggests, a café. Internet cafés have frequently developed as a response to the difficulties experienced by mobile users or visitors to an area in obtaining internet access. It is noticeable that in a few areas or countries with exceptionally good internet access, the internet café has been a passing phenomenon as the ubiquity of access reduces the commercial advantage of private businesses. In many rural and remote areas across the world, the internet café has frequently filled the role of a local **learning centre** for students who either lack access to computing facilities in their home, or lack access to specialised equipment (such as a **videoconference** unit) or specialist services (i.e. **broadband** access, or a particular piece of **software**).

The level of sophistication of an internet café may range from simply the basic provision of a self-service computer terminal with internet access, to a more highly managed facility that includes technical support and perhaps even basic skills training. Some suppliers have extended their services (particularly in urban areas) to cater for the mobile user by offering internet access via **wireless networks** that allow, for example, business users to conduct informal meetings over coffee in roadside cafés. The distinction between an internet café and a local learning centre is blurred, with the former being largely a facility for casual or occasional users, whereas a local learning centre generally has a more structured, regular, or formal approach. Some of the more elaborate internet cafés may become 'badged' as learning centres to add marketing value to their profile. An additional educational value of the internet café could be considered to be the social value of providing a gathering place for learners seeking remote access to educational provision, and this has been described as a 'third place' (after home and the workplace) by Oldenberg and others who stress the value of social interaction and group reinforcement that can be provided by learning **communities**, either **online** or in other 'third places' that provide a comfortable networking facility for learners.

Further reading

Oldenberg, R. (1989). *The great good place.* New York: Marlowe & Company.

INTERNET SERVICE PROVIDER (ISP)

A company that provides a user with a connection to the **internet**, usually for a cost, though universities and colleges are also internet service providers for their students. It is a common complaint from students that when they cease to be students they lose their access to the university/college ISP and therefore, in their search to find another ISP, frequently lose track of fellow students and access to institutional **online** learning **communities**.

INTRANET

A form of local area **network** (**LAN**) that connects the computer systems of a single organisation. An intranet is used to provide common services, such as **email**, access to a common pool of **software**, or corporate **webpages**, and uses the same basic structural concepts as the **internet**, with local **clients** and **servers**. An intranet may be connected to the internet (but this is not mandatory) in which case it will normally include a **firewall** to protect the local network from **virus** contamination by external sources. The more sophisticated intranets will allow for different sections to have a different status, e.g. there might be some open-access webpages to provide public guidance or advertising, while senior staff will have access to secure areas that are **password** protected, such as internal **email** and finance details. Due to the fact that different users can be given different levels of access permissions on an intranet, they can be used effectively to promote **collaborative work**, as well as providing a good base for sharing resources (computer applications, documents, **graphics**, or **databases**) as well as providing for **distributed education** in the workplace environment.

JAVA

A particular programming language that is designed to be cross-platform, i.e. it is compatible to run on a variety of computer operating systems, such as Microsoft Windows or Apple MacIntosh. It is currently particularly favoured for its use in constructing certain features of **webpages** (such as **animations** or **multimedia**) as programmers are able to write free-standing applications. These applications are then decoded and run by the machine that accesses the website, rather than the host **server**.

JPEG

An acronym for Joint Photographic Experts Group, identifying a specific type of file designed to compress photographs easily for transmission between computers in a **network**, such as the **internet**, or an **intranet**. JPEG files usually have the extension .jpg after the file name and are the most common format for the transfer of photographic files over the **web**. The method of compression is best suited for photographs, but not **icons** or other **graphics**, which are more suited to **GIF** format files.

KILLER APP

The 'killer application' has come to mean the 'next big thing' that will achieve a breakthrough to a new level of **ICT** use. It is derived from the observation that an innovative piece of **software** frequently provides the extra marketing incentive that encourages a mass of the public to purchase the supporting **hardware** e.g. a particular brand of computer, or in **games and gaming**, a particular brand of handset or control consul. The search for the next killer app has become the next 'best thing' of ICT companies, as widespread public adoption of a new application has frequently led to the generation of considerable wealth and prestige.

LAN

An abbreviation for a Local Area Network of computers, usually connecting up a few computers on a small scale, in the home or a workplace. Depending on its purpose, the LAN may or may not be able to connect with other **networks**, e.g. to form a part of the **internet**, by using a router to join wide area networks (WAN). A LAN may form an **intranet** when it is used solely within a single organisation.

LEARNING CENTRE

A facility offering access to learning resources (e.g. computers, **internet** access, library resources) that is usually located at some distance remote from the main teaching centre, college etc. They may vary widely in size, equipment and function from simply an office in another building (local school, Citizens Advice Bureau etc.) to a customised facility that offers more than just IT access. Local Learning Centres have a long tradition in some areas, especially rural localities where there have traditionally been difficulties in either accessing modern IT equipment or gaining reasonably fast access to the internet. In Scandinavia there was an early 'telecottage' movement that established a **network** of centres throughout rural and remote areas, and these frequently functioned as an 'electronic village hall' for the local community. Telecottages were equipped with a range of IT equipment and made available for communal use at a moderate charge, a sort of rural, community-owned business centre. Frequently they were also used to locate 'teleworkers', employees from one or more organisation or business who would 'telecommute' with the distant workplace using various methods of e-communications.

The idea spread to the Highlands and Islands of Scotland in the early 1990s and was adapted to suit a variety of formats. The UHI Millennium Institute has supported the development of a newer version through their network of over 110 local learning centres throughout the region, mostly in rural and remote locations (see Figure 6). The learning centres are intended to provide an academic environment for students who are unable to attend their host campus, which may be on another island, or many miles away. Learndirect, a clearing-house academic provider, has also been active in promoting the use of learning centres by students who are scattered in areas remote from their academic course provider. The standards of learning centres can vary widely, some simply offering a quiet place to study, with perhaps computing facilities and some 'social space'. The more sophisticated offer **broadband** internet access and **videoconference** facilities, as well as office resources such as photocopying or library handling. There is a move to attempt to classify learning centres on the level of provision that they offer in order to provide an indicator of equity in the facilities offered to students. As broadband access becomes more universally available, and as other IT applications rise to challenge relatively expensive solutions such as videoconferencing, it remains to be seen what the effect on learning centres might be. There may be a shift e.g. from IT provision to a greater role in providing social **interaction** for students, or learning centres may strengthen their role in the provision of specialist services such as library access or shared computing applications that demand a high level of site security. Some learning centres may also have 'caretaker' staff who are engaged to help students with any IT problems, and may even provide a (non-subject-specialist) academic **mentoring** role for students (e.g. dealing with generic academic issues).

On the whole learning centres are employed as drop-in facilities in areas of scattered population, but some also offer **face-to-face (f2f)** classes, or use their technology to host small groups of local students who

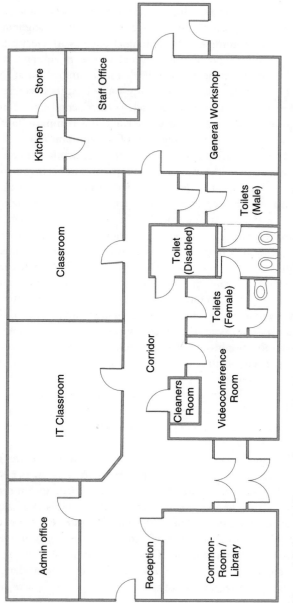

Figure 6 Schematic diagram of a purpose-built learning centre on the Isle of Barra (Re-drawn by Fiona Rennie)

are tutored by staff from another location in the network. In some cases learning centres may be used to register remote students, provide induction to their courses, offer video counselling services or guidance, and generally function as a local surrogate for the main academic campus delivering their course. Although there has been a history of colleges and universities supporting the development of a range of learning centres, the cost-effectiveness of delivering a quality service to small numbers of distributed learners has often proved difficult to sustain. More recently there have been moves to encourage ownership of local learning centres by community organisations, local authorities, and/or private providers, and the strength of this model is reflected in the estimation of the value to the local community of a facility that is seen to provide a tangible link with centres of learning that are located outwith the community itself

LEARNING MANAGEMENT SYSTEM (LMS)

A Learning Management System is synonymous with **MLE** or Managed Learning Environment and sometimes also with **VLE**, Virtual Learning Environment. LMS is the term favoured in the US and is often used for provision of corporate training. Whatever the term, the **software** provides a means of administering elearning by providing an access system as well as a tracking system for student progress. Of course facilities for communication, **assessment** and content display are also part of the **platform**.

LEARNING OBJECTS

Reusable Learning Objects (RLOs) or just LOs are small units of learning. They have several characteristics which account for the notion that they are a new way of thinking about learning. The first of these is that learning objects are self-contained, that is, they can be studied independently and do not normally refer to other learning objects. This factor leads to the next characteristic: they are reusable in any number of different contexts. LOs can be aggregated into whole courses and can be combined with traditional content. The third important feature of an LO is the use of **metadata**, or **metatagging**, wherein a set of descriptive information about the LO is provided so that **learning object repositories** can be easily searched for appropriate material.

What is the problem to which learning objects are the solution? Many academics think this is still an open question! The obvious answer is that the use of learning objects can reduce duplication of effort in course production. Elearning requires an increase in specially designed learning materials and high quality elearning material requires large student numbers or a sizeable budget in order to justify the cost. To address this problem, a number of national and international initiatives have developed to create digital repositories of learning objects. The vision is that publishers, teachers, support staff, commercial companies and even students would contribute learning objects which could then be easily accessed, recombined, adapted to different levels and educational models. Examples of such repositories are: CLOE, MERLOT, CAREO, Edutella, The Learning Object Federation. For details see the websites listed below.

Repositories are built on **database** technology, but they go beyond a simple storage device. Most encourage discovery, exchange and reuse. As their use expands, it has become apparent that a distributed model linking a range of repositories is a more appropriate scenario. LOs are likely to be stored in any number of places which are all linked by internet technology.

Unsurprisingly, there are a number of problems with the reuse of LOs and LO repositories:

1. The issue of combining content from multiple sources.
2. The challenge of developing such flexible content in the first place.
3. The availability of **platforms** to support such use.

In many respects the vision of LO reuse is a simplistic one, namely: teaching involves the transmission of short blocks of content, and learning is the acquisition of information. The educational process, in most Western universities at least, is much more complex, interactive and supported by human intervention. Learning objects, therefore, even when combined to form a whole course, are in effect a series of resources which need to be supported by activities, **interaction** with **tutors** and other students, and possibly non-digital learning resources. In addition the learning design of the course needs to be considered right from the start. Authoring tools that enable teachers to model their educational design in an **online** environment are currently being developed (see links below).

In order to be totally flexible, learning objects should be free of context. In theory that would mean, no reference to any specific discipline, teaching situation or level. This is almost a contradiction in terms, since good teaching is usually considered to be highly adapted to the specific students, subject and context. One solution to this dilemma is to separate the context from the content – not a process teachers are used to performing. This accounts for some of the resistance to learning object reuse by many educators.

In a sense the metadata attached to each learning object provides one level or type of context. One definition of a learning object is in fact, data plus context (that is, a resource plus metadata). LO metadata can record the level of difficulty of the resource, the subject matter and its relation to other LOs. If one exercise was designed to follow another, a good system can automatically provide links to it. While such complex systems are not readily available as yet, it is easy to see that reuse becomes more attractive.

To date it is generally acknowledged that reuse of learning objects is not widespread. Some claim that there is not a large enough pool of LOs across all subjects and levels. Others claim that even if such repositories were available, the object assembly model of course development, where the instructor puts a course together by drawing objects from a range of repositories, is not a pedagogically sound or even an efficient approach. Interspersing LOs into an otherwise conventional (online) course may well be the dominant use in future. LOs then become just another teaching resource. This is a far cry from the initial promise of LOs which was to take learning to new levels of personalisation and relevancy.

Web links

http://www.irrodl.org/content/v2.1/downes.html
http://www.educause.edu/LearningObjects/2601
http://jodi.ecs.soton.ac.uk/Articles/v03/i04/Polsani/

Further reading

Littlejohn, A. (ed.) (2003). *Reusing Online Resources*. A sustainable approach to e-learning. London: Kogan Page.
McGreal, R. (ed.) (2004). *Online Education Using Learning Objects*. London: RoutledgeFalmer.

LEARNING OBJECT REPOSITORIES

These are set up to facilitate the reuse of **learning objects**. Many different forms exist:

- Open repositories which promote sharing and exploration of knowledge and operate on a free-of-charge basis under open-content;

- Open-source licences, a credit system whereby virtual credits are awarded for objects that are used and reused the most;
- A micro-payment system.

Some repositories do not actually house the objects; they merely provide **metadata** about the object and links which point to it. Some repositories use a peer review system to evaluate the quality of the objects. There are subject specific repositories (http://turing.bear.uncw.edu/iLumina/index.asp), software repositories (http://www.edtechpost.ca/pmwiki/pmwiki.php/Main/LearningObjectRepositorySoftware), repositories for students (http://cnx.rice.edu/) and commercial repositories (http://xanedu.com/), as well as general repositories: Merlot (http://www.merlot.org/Home.po) Careo (http://careo.ucalgary.ca/cgi-bin/WebObjects/CAREO.woa).

A repository differs from standard **webpages** because it provides teachers and/or students with information that is structured and organised to facilitate the finding and use of learning materials regardless of their source location.

Web links

http://cloe.on.ca/
http://careo.ucalgary.ca/cgi-bin/WebObjects/CAREO.woa
http://www.merlot.org/Home.po
http://edutella.jxta.org/
http://thelearningfederation.org/

LIFELONG LEARNING

The European Union has defined Lifelong Learning in a very broad way to include all types of learning at all ages:

- It is about acquiring and updating all kinds of abilities, interests, knowledge and qualifications from the pre-school years to post-retirement. It promotes the development of knowledge and competencies that will enable each citizen to adapt to the knowledge-based society and actively participate in all spheres of social and economic life, taking more control of his or her future.
- It is about valuing all forms of learning, including: formal learning, such as a degree course followed at university; non-formal learning, such as vocational skills acquired at the workplace; and informal

learning, such as inter-generational learning, for example where parents learn to use **ICT** through their children, or learning how to play an instrument together with friends. From the learner's point of view, therefore, lifelong learning is a continuous engagement in acquiring and applying knowledge and skills in the context of authentic, self-directed problems. (http://europa.eu.int/comm/education/policies/lll/life/what_islll_en.html)

Several critical issues arise from this apparently simple statement about the nature of lifelong learning. These are:

1. Learning should take place in the context of authentic, complex problems, rather than learning as answers to someone else's questions.
2. Learning should be embedded in the pursuit of intrinsically rewarding activities.
3. Learning-on-demand needs to be supported because change is inevitable, it is impossible to cover any subject completely, and obsolescence is unavoidable.
4. Organisational and **collaborative** learning recognise the essentially social nature of learning.
5. Skills and processes that support learning as a lifetime habit must be developed.

These characteristics reflect very closely what we know about learning. The first thing we know is that the learner is not a receptacle into which knowledge can be poured. Rather, learners construct their understanding uniquely and actively. This of course is quite at odds with the dominant instructional model of much formal education which stresses additive content transmission. Second, learners develop different learning preferences, such that no one method of teaching will be equally effective for all learners. One way of coping effectively with this variation is to provide direct learning experiences so that each learner can engage with the subject in the way that is most suitable. We also know that learning occurs best in the context of a compelling problem – one that is specific and within the capacity of the learner to solve. In addition to this active engagement, learners need time for reflection. The challenge of solving problems produces a major surge in short-term neural activity. Building lasting cognitive connections, however, requires periods of reflective activity. Finally, effective learning needs a supportive social milieu and frequent opportunities for peer **interaction** and **feedback**. Consequently, both universities and schools need to move beyond seeing their mission as teaching facts and providing information, towards a much more challenging mission of teaching people how to learn and motivating them to do this throughout their lives.

Learning to learn has always been the Holy Grail of the education process and as such, has always been more preached about than practised. The updated and arguably more urgently needed requirement now is the ability to elearn, that is, to learn using the facilities and affordances of the **online** environment. It is more urgent in that the need to learn facts and information has vastly reduced and the ability to find, manipulate, analyse, synthesise and re-purpose information has increased concomitantly. One of the key resources in developing these abilities is other people. Gone are the old threats that machines will replace teachers; machines can store, link and process information, but people transform it and add value to it. **Tutors**, mentors, **moderators** and online **facilitators** are now seen as the asset that makes all the difference to student **retention, motivation** and acceptance of elearning. Likewise, CBT (**computer-based training**) put up on the **Web** with no human support, is increasingly seen as unsuccessful and a 'horseless-carriage' use of connectivity. Because there is so much information available on the net, what is valued is knowing how to cope with it. Connecting with other people to share the load, to exchange tips and models for managing information, and to express ideas and give feedback, has become an essential element of elearning methodology. Fundamentally this kind of learning rests on the understanding that the technology is *a* tool, not *the* tool.

The ability to use computers and other technology to improve learning, productivity and performance, is a general definition of technology literacy. In fact, openness to new technologies and the willingness to try out new **software** and new communications opportunities are more important than expertise with a wide range of software. What we are witnessing in advanced Western countries is an upsurge in individuals realising the benefits of networked computing *themselves*, and through pursuing their own interests, hobbies and contacts, finding a whole new vehicle for effective learning – informally.

European policy makes a distinction between non-formal and informal learning based on the intention of the learner: informal learning results from activities in daily life at work, at home, at leisure; non-formal learning is intentional on the part of the learner and structured in terms of learning objectives, but is not accredited by a recognised education or training institution. In reality, most analysts admit that the boundaries between formal, non-formal and informal learning are blurred and can only be meaningfully drawn in relation to particular contexts. It is more useful to talk about dimensions of formality and to look at ways in which these aspects interrelate.

While online **communities** are being exploited by universities and schools, informal learning through online communities is a much larger phenomenon. Online communities can be categorised in a number of ways. One of these is:

- Geographic – defined by a physical location like a city or region;
- Demographic – defined by age, gender, race or nationality;
- Topical – defined by shared interest, like a fan club, hobby group or professional organisation;
- Activity-based – defined by a shared activity like shopping, investing, playing **games** or making music.

Arguably the most significant area of online community resulting in informal learning outcomes is the health sector. Informal learners who go online for health-related information want several things: to understand their problems better; to find information about diseases and treatments; to get support from others; to help fellow sufferers; to feel less afraid and so on. Websites offer some information, but online communities are more personal resources.

Another example of informal learning is referred to as '**edutainment**', in the form of the plethora of semi-educational games which are available. The application of connected electronic games environments to 'real life' educational events, including general election results, in-depth news coverage, online **simulations** and military or medical training illustrate just some of the informal opportunities for learning not previously available. Online, informal opportunities to learn while playing are a phenomenon that cannot be ignored. Games are changing the nature of learning and affecting attention spans; they demand multi-tasking, and experiential and collaborative activity.

ICT is producing a major change in both the content and the processes of learning. Belonging to a range of **networks** is an informal strategy of increasing opportunities for lifelong learning. Professional updating courses offer another, more obvious opportunity. Self-initiated learning, using both online and offline resources, is a non-formal means of developing expertise in a chosen area.

LOGON/OFF OR LOGIN/OUT

This is the act of joining and/or leaving a computer system or a **network**, usually by typing a specific user identification (or 'user name') and a corresponding **password** known only to the individual user (and the system administrator.) Once a user has logged on to a computer system the system will 'recognise' the individual user and accord them specific system privileges and constraints (e.g. students will gain access to approved student resources, but not to staff areas; students may be able to access the **internet**, or the **intranet**, and search certain **online libraries**). For this reason it is important that when a user is finished working with the system then s/he should log off as a user, otherwise the next person to use that computer could assume their online identity and gain access to personal files or restricted areas of the network.

LURKING

A derogatory term for people who read messages on computer conferences and/or **discussion boards** but do not contribute themselves. **Online** facilitators are always encouraging students to actively engage with the discussion, on the understanding that students will benefit from trying to express their thoughts and getting **feedback** on them from others. Nevertheless, lurking has been shown to be useful in some contexts and with some kinds of learners.

MENTAL MODELS

These are internal pictures or metaphors we create, often unconsciously to help us understand how things work. A good example of a visual metaphor is the directory structure of a computer as presented by MS-Window's Explorer program. While the computer actually stores files and data haphazardly on its hard drive, the visual metaphor presented to the user is that of file folders and a vertical ordering system. This metaphor gives an artificial but clear sense of order to the system. As users we imagine that our documents are being held in these little folders, and that there is some kind of 'depth' to them.

MENTORING

As part of the process of **distributed education**, and more generally in respect of elearning and the delivery of educational provision to learners who are at locations remote from their **tutor**, the appointment of a local staff contact, or mentor, is frequently encouraged. The mentor need not be an academic in the same field as the learner, and in fact may not currently be an active academic as their main function is to provide generic support that is not necessarily discipline-based. A mentor will generally act as a point of local contact for a learner remote from the main campus, providing more than simply pastoral guidance, but not actually teaching or **tutoring** in the particular subject field of the learner. As such, a mentor will frequently provide a service for learners covering a range of disciplines, e.g. the various users of a local **learning centre**, or may be the appointed contact for the provision of **face-to-face (f2f)** guidance for a single class on a multi-campus institution where the tuition is being provided from another campus.

The mentor will commonly deal with very broad learning issues such as ensuring that learners are able to access their **MLE** from the learning centre, or that the **videoconference** connections are correctly established and they may for instance invigilate for exams at appropriate times. Skills such as essay writing, correct citations for references, and even basic diagnosis of literacy/ numeracy deficiencies may be provided locally to learners by the mentor, who acts as a low level academic support for the main tutorial team. Commonly the mentor will maintain close contacts with the student advisor for the course. The main function of the mentor is to support the system of distributed education by providing, as part of a wider team, general learner support and guidance that is also distributed around the **network**. Normally a mentor would not be considered a part of the core academic team, but rather is an integral member of the learner support services that are so crucial to the creation of a sense of learning **community** among distributed learners, which in turn promotes better learner engagement, **interaction** and course **retention**.

META TAG

The meta tag is used by search engines to allow them to more accurately list a site in their indexes. Meta tags are descriptive words in a website code which help search engines identify the main topics of a website.

METADATA

The term for information about a **learning object** that enables it to be stored and retrieved from a **database**. It is information about the learning object, not information in the learning object. In short, it is data about the data. Learning Object Metadata (LOM) provides information about the attributes and format of the learning object e.g. title, author, date, educational context and intent. Both **meta tags** and metadata are essential to control work flow and output of information from the repository.

MLE

A Managed Learning Environment (*see* **VLE**).

MODEM

This word has come to signify a device connected to a computer that **mod**ulates and **dem**odulates the digital data produced by a computer and encodes this as analogue data for transfer through an ordinary telephone line, to be decoded at the other end into digital data and read by another computer system. The modem was a necessary device to allow dial-up **email** and any **internet** connection before the arrival of digital telephone lines and **broadband** access to the internet. Although still common, their use is likely to become redundant for normal connections as digital connections become more commonplace, though there may still be a use for them in certain specialised situations such as separating multiple signals in wireless transmissions and in making use of domestic power lines to also carry broadband internet data.

MODERATOR

Sometimes called 'emoderator', the moderator is a person who presides over **online** conferences and **discussion boards**. In the context of elearning, the moderator is usually the **tutor**. The primary function of the moderator is facilitating the online discussions. This means any or all of the following:

1. Choosing the topic for discussion.
2. **Posting** questions strategically to keep the discussion going.
3. Encouraging **interactivity** with students in the topic through adding background information, sharing relevant anecdotes.
4. Modelling the kind of responses expected from students especially synthesising and summarising messages.
5. Pointing to outside resources, **URLs**, articles or books as sources of information on the topic.

6. Sending **email** to students privately if they are contributing too much or not enough.
7. Acknowledging good inputs from students.
8. Weaving together discussion threads and summarising at the end of the discussion.

The moderator may have a number of administrative duties such as setting up new discussion areas, technical duties such as answering IT queries and/or **assessment** responsibilities. The role is usually heaviest at the beginning of the course when students need a lot of support and confidence-building, and the moderator needs to set the tone of the discussions. Turn-taking is an important skill to encourage in the group as is the ability to express opinions without being overbearing. The job has often been likened to a good host of a party.

MODULE

A short structured part of a course of academic study. There is a great deal of variation from one educational provider to another in the size or length of a module. In general terms there has been a tendency in recent years to divide the academic year more flexibly into a number of related units or blocks (or modules) of related study topics. Some educational providers allow learners to choose to study modules independently as free-standing short courses. A typical module might last for the duration of one semester, or term, and would necessitate 100–150 hours of study, possibly by means of **distributed education** or other study modes that provide a level of flexibility for learners. A number of modules on related themes can be grouped together (by the institution and/or the learner) to form a recognised course of study, leading to the achievement of an academic award. This building block of the module has the advantage that learners can combine a few modules together for an award, or progress to collecting a few more modules for a higher award, and so on. Each module is on a discrete academic topic and may be assessed independently of any other modules.

MOO/MUD

These terms are frequently used interchangeably to refer to a Multi-User Domain, a concept derived from **games and gaming**, that allows users a high level of **interactivity** in performing certain tasks. A MOO is a

MUD that is 'object oriented' and allows users to construct the environment of the domain using **role play** and a **database** to create a form of **virtual reality**, e.g. by constructing rooms, buildings, objects, landscapes and other elements of a virtual **online** environment. A MUD/MOO may offer the users the option of constructing **avatars** to represent themselves online, and to some extent have been used in elearning to create a **simulation** of a learning activity that is difficult, dangerous, or prohibitively expensive to construct in real life.

MOTIVATION

The disposition and commitment of the learner to learn, in other words, motivation, is considered to be the most important factor influencing learning effectiveness. Motivation to learn may be defined as those factors that energise and direct behavioural patterns organised around a learning goal. There are two sets of factors which are included in the notion of motivation: extrinsic and intrinsic factors. Extrinsic factors originate in external structures and reward. For example, pay, professional standards, organisational policies and norms as well as requirements originating in formal learning programmes where the individual is enrolled. Intrinsic factors stem from inner or self-driven pressures to grow and achieve, and thus include personal desires, the need to conform, the quest for esteem and challenges such as solving problems or supporting others. In terms of elearning, research has shown that intrinsically motivated participants are relatively more explorative and do qualitatively different things **online**. This finding has been confirmed through students' self-reported inclination to explore the environment.

MULTIMEDIA

A term that is often used very loosely and therefore has decreasing academic value. In general it is used to describe the bringing together of a variety of different media to create a rich learning environment e.g. **webpages** with **audio/video clips** embedded, accompanied by printed learning resources and an **email** or **audioconference** link. The progressive **convergence** of digital devices, (such as computers, personal digital assistants (PDAs) and mobile telephones) has allowed a greater scope and diversity of multimedia opportunities for education, and to some extent has reduced its novelty.

MULTIPLE CHOICE QUESTION (MCQ)

This is a form of **assessment** in which the learner is presented with a statement or question, and a number of different responses, only one of which is correct, with the other 'answers' being plausible, but incorrect (distractors). MCQs are a form of objective test, that is, they are designed to enable the marker to assess the knowledge of the learner without exercising any subjective judgement on its value. Although they have been criticised by some educationalists for only assessing a superficial level of knowledge, MCQs are frequently included in the **course design** of elearning **modules** as self-test, or formative assessments to allow the learner to evaluate his/her understanding of the topic and measure progress. The inclusion of MCQs on more sophisticated **VLE** or **MLE** allows the **tutor**, not simply to provide a yes/no response, but to give immediate **feedback** to the learner. This feedback may be in the form of an explanation for the incorrect choice, or it may provide deeper layers of information to more fully explain the reason for the correct or incorrect choice (e.g. a **hyperlink** to another **webpage** with detailed **case studies**, or to an academic article on the topic in an **online library**. Although well designed MCQs require time and skill to construct, they have the advantage that they then function automatically (without tutor intervention) and are suitable for **asynchronous learning** and **distributed education** activities. Some complex MCQs will allow for the random selection of questions from a 'question bank', and will adjust the level of questions presented to the learner in relation to their level of performance (i.e. presenting harder questions if the learner seems to be finding them too easy, or providing easier questions when the learner continually fails to make the correct choice.)

The facilities of the **web** have allowed MCQ developers to use **multimedia** and a wide variety of question types. For example:

- True/false questions;
- Assertion-reason questions (combining elements of MCQ and true/false);
- Multiple-response questions (involving the selection of more than one answer from a list and picking from a list of options x, y, z, etc.);
- Text/numerical questions (involving the input of text or numbers at the keyboard);
- Ranking questions (requiring students to relate items in a column to one another, thus testing the knowledge of the order of events);
- Sequencing questions (requiring the student to position text in a given sequence, which is particularly good for testing methodology.

NETIQUETTE

A common term for 'network etiquette' or the 'rules of engagement' for **online** practitioners. Due to the brief and sometimes terse nature of **email** and messages to **discussion boards** or other **computer conferencing** applications, it is very easy to offend other users unintentionally. On some occasions giving offence may lead to **flaming** while more generally it will simply discourage **interaction** between learners and a lessening of **trust** in the members of online **communities**. Netiquette is a response aimed at minimising these negative aspects by providing at the outset a clear set of guidelines on how online users should show consideration for other users. Simple indications of the tone of the message, or the intention of the user can be given by the incorporation of **emoticons** in the text to suggest humour, irony etc. or by indicating emphasis by SHOUTING in capitals to stress KEY words.

More generally, as in other walks of life, it is helpful to imagine yourself in the shoes of the other person. If offence is accidentally caused by a message that is misinterpreted, users should not be slow to apologise and correct the error. Generally speaking regular online users are pretty tolerant of short, to-the-point messages and bad spelling, but they will be less tolerant if they are required to waste time with irrelevant email, repetitive bad manners, or actions that cause them to lose performance on their computer (such as sending complex files or large images). Etiquette includes simple rules such as 'don't copy an embarrassing message to a third party without the consent of the original sender'. Avoid using offensive, rude, or racist language and try to avoid inconveniencing other users by actions such as attaching large files that **modem** users will find slow or impossible to **download**.

Take care not to clog up users email accounts by distributing unwanted messages as a result of 'copying to all' rather than simply copying to the person who was intended, and basically show a little common courtesy to other online users. As a rule **computer mediated communications** afford opportunities to read users' messages, pause, reflect offline, and then return online to **post** a reply that is carefully considered and appropriate. Breaches of netiquette most frequently occur when users give rapid-fire responses to online comments that they later regret when they have had time to cool down. Good elearning courses normally devote some induction time at the start of the course to issues of netiquette, procedures for communicating with **tutors** and general online protocol.

Web links

http://www.albion.com/netiquette

NETMEETING

This is a proprietorial **software** application that enables a form of **desktop videoconferencing** between individual computers as well as sharing other communication tools. Using an **internet** connection a user can dial another user and share a **chat** space for **synchronous** discussion, either one-to-one or one-to-many. The user may also have the use of audio connection, but depending on the quality of the microphone and the connection it may be clearer to use a telephone in combination. The addition of a **webcam** will enable **synchronous** video images to be exchanged, and this can create a powerful experience of learning and sharing, allowing body (facial) language to be seen and other emotions that permit the subtle exchange of human expressions, humour, confusion, etc. Normally video exchange is one-to-one whereas the synchronous exchange of **text messages** in the **chatroom** can be one-to-many, enabling a **tutor** to conduct a synchronous discussion with a whole class. This text dialogue can be saved and archived for further use. Some more recent versions of this type of application allow for a small number of multiple screens of synchronous video.

Netmeeting has other sharing facilities, such as a whiteboard, file transfer and the ability to share desktops. The latter function allows a tutor to take control of the desktop of a student (or colleague) so that the screen of both computers appears exactly the same. The user in control can then navigate with their own mouse through an activity, such as **surfing** for a **web** site, editing a document, or displaying figures in a spreadsheet, and what they see on their screen will also be seen simultaneously by the user with the shared desktop. Control can be swapped between users, creating a powerful collaboration tool for **peer-to-peer** working and for sharing learning resources as a form of **distributed education**. This application has the ability to combine a number of different collaboration tools and to allow the user to work normally from their own computer with a remote colleague, but due to its method of connecting to the internet, some users may experience difficulty in connecting due to the blocking effects of the **firewall** of their institution.

NETWORKS

The ability to join two or more computer systems together to exchange information has led to the establishment of various types of computer networks, including the Local Area Network (**LAN**), the Wide Area Network (WAN), and ultimately the **internet** through which many of these networks are globally linked. With respect to elearning, the terms 'network learning' and 'network courses' have arisen from the ability to link geographically scattered learners together in one 'class' to benefit from techniques of **distributed education**. Networks can function for either **synchronous** or **asynchronous learning**, depending upon the **software** applications being used and the educational purpose of the connection. The **peer–to–peer** connections can be used for student support, as well as **collaborative work**, and as a means of facilitating educational **interaction** among the members of the network.

ONLINE

The activity of being engaged in using a computer **network**, such as the **internet** or an **intranet**, for sending/receiving **email**, using a **browser** to search the **web**, and/or for transferring files from one computer to another. To get online the user is normally required to **logon** with a unique user identification and self-selected **password**, then select a **software** application to connect to the relevant network. The fact that so much **interaction** can take place during this networked activity has given rise to the word 'online' being used extensively as a descriptive prefix for many other activities and concepts, such as 'online learning' as a synonym for elearning, 'online personality' for the **avatar** or the characteristic personal traits that the user chooses to display while networking, or '**online libraries**' for the literature, images and other resources that are available over the internet. In contrast 'offline' is frequently used to describe work or activities that are prepared in advance when the user is not online, then **uploaded**, or transferred to another location by 'cutting-and-pasting' or as an **attachment** during an online connection, rather than spending time (and money) typing long messages 'live' while online.

ONLINE LIBRARIES

This is developing as a generic term for **online** access to a range of library resources and is becoming a key component of **blended learn-**

ing approaches to higher education. Sometimes called 'hybrid libraries' the initial concept was to have online access to the catalogue of a distant library, but this has expanded rapidly with the availability of digital resources and online journals. Allied to the concept of **Lifelong Learning** in which people are encouraged to participate in **flexible learning** throughout their lives, online libraries are growing in popularity as a partial solution to encouraging **accessibility** to appropriate learning resources. This is closely allied to **distributed learning**, whereby education can be delivered to individuals and **communities** wherever they are located. As elearning has encouraged the spread of learners in off-campus sites, of necessity the need has grown to provide adequate library resources on an equitable basis to students who may be many miles (or hours) away from a conventional paper-based academic library.

Online libraries now include gateway sites (**portals**) that provide a single link to a list, sometimes searchable, of other identified useful sources of information. These lists may link to another **webpage**, or an online academic journal through commercial services such as BIDS, Infotrac, or EBSCO providing abstracts and/or full-text articles. Increasingly, as with 'conventional libraries', the online library may contain links to sources of digital images, sound files (e.g. guidance commentary or interviews), **video clips**, ebooks, data sets and other forms of digitally stored materials. In some specific subject areas librarians and course **tutors** may have gathered together selected resources on a subject, such as by **digitising** articles from journals or chapters from books under a **copyright** licence agreement. As more material is being made available digitally to access over the **internet**, some observers have suggested that the **digital divide** of the future will not just be between those people who have access to the internet, but in reality between those who are e-literate, that is, able to search, identify, select and re-use digital information from elibraries and other online repositories.

An increasing number of university and college libraries provide orientation guides for their learners in the form of subject guides to online resources accessible through their own institutional webpages. Under such systems course teams can build up sets of digital resources that can be carefully tailored to the needs of learners on specific courses and/or **modules** of courses with copyright clearance for a certain number of learners and duration. Key benefits of this system are in being able to provide quality materials directly to the desk of learners, particularly learners in rural, remote and/or international locations; the repository is easily maintained and quickly updated, and can include copies of rare and fragile documents, or materials now out of print. With the addition of sound and image files it is possible to customise a **multimedia** range of resources to enhance the learning experience, and this can be provided at various levels of depth for each individual subject, e.g. as backup notes for a session in a module, or more detailed resources for learners who want to go into more depth, or even as a specialist option for higher level students and researchers.

Web links

Library of Congress online: http://www.loc.gov/wiseguide/index-flash.html
Example: http://www.questia.com/Index.jsp
Article: http://www5.oclc.org/downloads/community/elearning.pdf

OPEN LEARNING

Open learning is a philosophy of education that values more opportunity for learners to engage in various ways with the educational process, not just through **face-to-face** (**f2f**) interaction. The term is used most commonly in the UK. In Australia the equivalent is referred to as **flexible learning**. Some commentators claim that there is no one definition of open learning; rather, there are a range of elements which could be included in a definition. For example:

- Location – students and teacher may be in different locations;
- Time – **interaction** can be in real time or more likely **asynchronous**;
- Entry qualifications – usually less stringent than for campus universities;
- Technology – a range of media may be used to support the delivery of the course, from large scale industrialised processes to small group teaching;
- Communication – can be face-to-face or more likely technology-mediated. Alternatively it can be a mixture of both.

The educational philosophy of open learning is usually learner-centred and the educational institution attempts to remove barriers that impede access to traditional courses. Usually, institutions offer choice over some of the following:

- medium or media, whether print, online, television or video;
- place of study, whether at home, in the workplace or on campus;

- pace of study, whether closely paced or unstructured;
- support mechanisms, whether **tutors** on demand, **audioconferences** or computer-assisted learning; and
- entry and exit points.

In short, educational provision can be called open learning according to the degree to which the institution is course-centred or learner-centred; and to the degree of flexibility existing in the areas such as admission policies, examination requirements, curriculum modifications and delivery methods.

OPEN SOURCE

This refers to **software** that has a freely available source code (the programming language) which is available to the public at no cost. The software should be distributed freely and include all relevant documentation. Programmers are able to rewrite and improve on the software, but are normally expected to return their improvements into the public domain at no charge. Some educational establishments have moved towards using open source software as the **platform** to operate their virtual learning environment (**VLE**) (or more correctly, Managed Learning Environment – **MLE**) on the grounds that they can avoid paying commercial licence fees to the suppliers, and are better able to customise the MLE to their specific requirements. On the other hand, not having a supplier to maintain the MLE means that the institution itself must incur the costs of running and developing their platform. In some cases, although the software itself is distributed at no cost, some companies offer commercial services to install and maintain the system on behalf of an institution. Advantages of using open source materials include the ability to select and change the appearance and functionality of the MLE and the ability to have a major influence on the future design of the system. This may be a major consideration, for example, when customising the VLE or MLE to allow for working in a minority language.

Examples of an open source VLE would include: Moodle http://moodle.org and Boddington http://bodington.org/index.jsp
The Open Source definition: http://opensource.org/docs/definition_plain.php
Article on Open Source: http://www.oreilly.com/catalog/opensources/book/perens.html

PASSWORD

A unique identifying combination of letters, numbers and/or symbols that is used in combination with a specific user name to identify an individual person and allow them access to secure sections of the **internet**. Passwords are commonly used to enable learners to enter **MLEs** (or **VLEs**) and **chatrooms**, as well as to send **email** and **instant messaging** communications.

PDF

The abbreviation for Portable Document Format that describes a file format developed by the **software** company Adobe Systems to create and save documents that can be transferred across **networks** to other computers. The value of a PDF file is that it can be viewed in the style of the original document, regardless of the software or **hardware** used by either the sender or receiver. A PDF file may contain text and/or **graphics**, and may be very simple or very complex, but the formatting retains the original look of the documents. A number of readers are available for different operating systems and can be **downloaded** free over the **internet**.

PEER–TO–PEER

A reference to the **interaction** between learners for mutual learning and support (or indeed between staff members in a form of supportive **collaborative work**.) The adoption of **constructivism** as a pedagogy for elearning encourages learners to build upon their experiences in order to put their learning into context. The ability to **network** learners in a **VLE** or **MLE** allows learners to share their experiences and to learn from each other as well as from the course **tutor**. Some of the more imaginative forms of academic **assessment** include peer–to–peer monitoring and marking of work done by other students, including written assignments, presentations and/or project work. Peer–to–peer support and **collaborative** working lends itself very well to a diversity of communication media (e.g. **videoconference, email, discussion boards** etc.) and is ideally suited for **distributed education**.

PEER ASSESSMENT

The process of a learner marking an **assessment** of another learner, for the purposes of **feedback** and/or as a contribution to the final grade, is known as peer assessment. Peer assessment is also used amongst academic staff members to comment on the work of other staff colleagues. Peer assessment may be formative (for the purposes of ongoing improvement) or summative (for a final grade). It has the benefit that in addition to the normal value of gaining feedback on the quality of submitted work, the person who is marking the work gains experience in assessing the critical points in the work of someone at their own level, thereby becoming more critically aware of the subject matter. Peer assessment has been used in elearning as a means of prompting **interaction** among learners, often using a **VLE** and/or a **discussion board** in order to share the comments with other learners and involve them more fully in the process of understanding what is meant by quality work at the appropriate level. Peer assessment can be regarded as a form of **peer-to-peer** learning and/or **collaborative work** that is structured around an academic **module** or course. In attempting to incorporate peer assessment as a formal part of elearning it will be necessary to clearly define in advance the specific nature/aims of the assessment, the marking scheme by which merit is awarded, and the criteria for pass or fail etc. These definitions need to be shared with both the examined and the examiners, and this process in itself can be utilised as a beneficial learning activity for all learners in benchmarking elements of **quality assurance**.

PLAGIARISM

The act of plagiarism occurs when a person passes off the words or ideas of another person as their own. The fault lies not in the use of the words or ideas, but in presenting them as something new and original, rather than derived from an existing source. Institutions vary in the seriousness with which they deal with plagiarism: some consider it theft and police students' work through surveillance and plagiarism detection **software**. An alternative approach is to combine smart assignment design with teaching students what plagiarism is, how to reference sources and why academic honesty matters.

The reason that plagiarism has risen to prominence as a major academic problem, is partly that plagiarism has become so easy with the proliferation of **internet** sites and partly that the distinction between publicly and privately owned information has blurred. The concept of ownership of physical property is well established. The notion of intellectual property is not nearly so well accepted. People who would never consider stealing records or tapes from a music shop, often do not have the same compunction about **peer-to-peer** file sharing of music. Furthermore, the seemingly public nature of so much **online** content masks the true ownership issues. Electronic resources are so easily reproduced that there exists a collective amnesia about intellectual property rights over internet material. Students who might have reservations about copying words and ideas from a book without acknowledgement, are less concerned about doing the same from internet sites.

The problem has been exacerbated by the growth of online paper mills that exist solely for the purpose of providing students with essays and homework solutions. Students may select from large **databases** of essays and solutions or they may pay to have something customised for their particular use. There are hundreds of such sites on the internet and many are profitable ventures.

For students working in a second language, the excuse is that 'the original author explained it so much better than they could'. Turning something that is well written into faltering language seems to them a foolish and retrograde step.

At a more general level, students often ask 'How can words and ideas be stolen? Surely we are all reusing others' ideas all the time'. With the rise of interest in **learning objects** and re-versioning course content, there is a movement away from instructors writing new material from scratch. It is doubly ironic therefore that academics are being encouraged to reuse content, but students are condemned for it! The fact is that legally, it is still considered plagiarism even when the ideas have been put into different words. If the original source of the ideas is not acknowledged, it is plagiarism.

Teachers are now being encouraged to take positive action to prevent plagiarism by integrating discussion about it into seminars, by creating assignments that discourage plagiarism and encourage original thinking, and by pointing to different types of plagiarism, in particular plagiarism from the internet. The internet has various guidelines for students on how to avoid unintentional plagiarism, tips on how to cite references correctly, and suggestions for developing good research and writing skills.

As this schemata from http://www.neiu.edu/~ejhowens/plagiarism/ shows, there are many gradations of plagiarism.

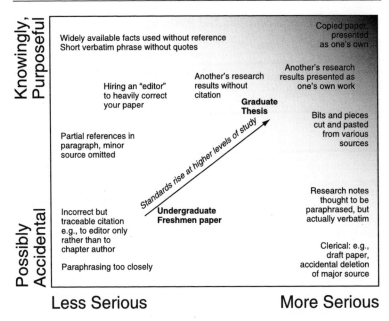

Figure 7 Gradations of plagiarism

There are several things that teachers can do to prevent plagiarism:

1. In larger classes, teachers might insist on a research trail which becomes part of the submitted paper. Or they could demand a research plan which makes use of the library. Alternatively they could ask for all the original handwritten notes, marked photocopies or printouts, and copies of all computer disk files. The research plan and the student's use of them could be a formal part of the project.
2. In small classes, the research process should be part of the assignment and made available to others in the group. Students can be asked to comment on each others research proposals. These occasions can be a major learning opportunity as workable and unworkable proposals are discussed, as well as interesting and trite ones.

Most plagiarism detection software is designed to detect material cut and pasted from the internet. For large classes, there is software that detects identical or very similar submissions. Some software will compile databases of submissions so that new work can be compared with earlier work. The threat of using plagiarism detection software is often enough to deter students.

Web links

http://bedfordstmartins.com/technotes/techtiparchive/
ttip102401.htm
http://online.northumbria.ac.uk/faculties/art/information_studies/
Imri/Jiscpas/site/pubsreps.asp
http://online.northumbria.ac.uk/faculties/art/information_studies/
Imri/Jiscpas/site/res_essay.asp
http://www.library.ualberta.ca/guides/plagiarism/

Further reading

Harris, R. (2001). *The Plagiarism Handbook: Strategies for Preventing, Detecting, and Dealing with Plagiarism*, Los Angeles, CA: Pyrczak Publishing.

PLATFORM

The term platform in elearning refers to the framework of **hardware** and/or **software** that enables a computer to run and interact with users. Usually this means the type of operating system of the computer **network**, though it is sometimes (erroneously) used to refer to the framework of the **VLE** architecture with which users interact. Quite simply, the platform is synonymous with the computer operating system that enables users to host other forms of computer software.

PORTAL

A website that offers a broad array of resources and services particularly geared for users new to that topic. A portal also provides a single point of access to a range of heterogeneous material brought together from more than one source. The term is synonymous with gateway. Typical services offered by public portal sites include a directory of **web** sites, a facility to search for other sites, news, weather information, **email**, stock quotes, phone and map information, and sometimes a **hyperlink** to related **communities** that meet **online**. The most common features on a university portal are: search facility, library administration and alerts, access to teaching material, personal information, campus news, institutional email and student handbook. There are a number of useful elearning portals:

Web links

http://e-learning.start4all.com/
http://www.elearn.govt.nz/elearn/elearn.portal
http://www.e-learningcentre.co.uk

POST OR POSTING

Members of online **communities** can send an electronic message to other members of their community by sending the equivalent of an **email** to a common **discussion board**, and this message appears on the discussion board as a posting. Students would therefore be encouraged to post their comments on a particular topic for further discussion, usually by sending short electronic messages, but perhaps also by including an **attachment** with some large piece of the students' work for comment or for **assessment**. Successive postings build up over a period of time as an **asynchronous** discussion on the course work by a group of learners who perhaps never meet **face-to-face** (**f2f**) due to the fact that they are separated by distance or time constraints.

PROBLEM-BASED LEARNING (PBL)

A learner-centred educational method that challenges students to 'learn to learn', working either individually or cooperatively in groups to seek solutions to real world problems. These problems are used to engage students' curiosity and motivate them to learn the subject matter. PBL prepares students to think critically and analytically, and to find and use appropriate learning resources. PBL aims to produce independent learners who can continue to learn on their own in life and in their chosen careers. The responsibility of the teacher in PBL is to provide the educational materials and guidance that facilitate learning. PBL is based on real world problems which are often messy and complex, and are aimed at ensuring recall and application to future problems. The PBL process is **learner-centered** at every step. Learning through exploring problem situations is not unique to elearning; in fact problem-based learning was popularised in the 1960s as a result of research with medical students at McMaster University in Canada. The research stemmed from a desire to develop in medical students the ability to relate the knowledge they had learned to the problems presented by patients, something that few medical students could do well.

What the research highlighted was a clear difference between problem-solving and problem-based learning. In the latter, problem scenarios are used to encourage students to engage themselves in the learning process; PBL is an educational format that is centred around the discussion and learning that emanates from a clinically based problem. It is a method that encourages independent learning and gives students practice in tackling puzzling situations and defining their own gaps in understanding in the context of relevant clinical problems, hopefully making it more likely that they will be able to recall the material later in the clinical setting. It is a way of learning that encourages a deeper understanding of the material rather than superficial coverage.

Yet the attraction of problem-based learning and its uptake in the 1970s and 1980s in Canada, Australia and the US, and in the late 1980s in the UK, seemed to lie not only in its timely emergence in relation to other worldwide changes in higher education, but also because of new debates about professional education. These related to a growing recognition that there needed to be not just a different view of learning and professional education, but also a different view about relationships between industry and education, between learning and society and between government and universities. Problem-based learning has been a huge area of growth in the UK, particularly in the last five years, and as yet there has been relatively little provision of resources to support its implementation, development and research.

QUALITY ASSURANCE

Questions about quality in elearning are constantly being raised and yet there is little agreement about what constitutes high quality. This is because 'fitness for purpose' is the ultimate determinant of quality. What is an outstandingly good course in one context is unsuccessful in another because the whole learning situation is different. Quality is one of those things that is hard to define but 'you know it when you see it'. The term 'quality assurance' usually has overtones of checking and evaluating to determine compliance with specific requirements or learning outcomes. The term 'quality enhancement' is what is considered when, for example, a programme previously taught **face-to-face (f2f)** is transformed for the **online** environment.

A number of quality assurance guidelines have been developed for elearning, some derived from campus teaching, others developed specifically for the online environment. The areas covered in such guidelines are usually similar: **course design** and **tutoring** processes, student services, technology and course delivery processes.

Course design and tutoring

Benchmarks of quality for course design focus on the stated learning outcomes and the way in which the course content flows from these. Similarly, the **assessment** processes should reflect all of the learning outcomes offering students opportunities to demonstrate their level of mastery of each one. The quality of online tutoring is critical to students achieving the learning outcomes. Requirements of high quality online **tutors** include the obvious ones such as depth of knowledge of the subject area, and presentation and organisational skills. In addition the interest, willingness and ability to interact with students online and to provide **feedback** and guidance are vital attributes. The quality of **interaction** with the tutor is one of the key indicators in many student surveys about elearning.

Student services

This domain can be subdivided into the services needed before registration, support during the learning experience, and the continued connection between learners and the institution after the particular course or program has been completed. Access to support materials e.g. how to be an elearner, how to use the elearning **platform** or **online libraries** should be developed as generic university services.

Technology

The **platform** for the delivery of elearning, both the course content and the interactions, must provide security and privacy of data and communication as a basic minimum. Prior notice of the downtime for maintenance is an important consideration, as are the processes and personnel needed to handle unanticipated technical problems. A telephone **help-desk** to answer students' queries and an online conference and set of **FAQs** for common problems are all facilities of high quality elearning provision. The extent to which administrative processes, such as registration, monitoring, counselling or complaints are handled online will depend on the individual educational institution. An online system for submission of assignments is one platform component that is an important feature of elearning provision.

Course delivery processes

Robust systems for handling a range of course delivery issues are required when teaching takes place online rather than face-to-face. Student handbooks, course guides and a course calendar need to be prepared and put online before the students **log on**. Library resources need to be identified, **copyright** cleared if necessary, and the materials made available online. Monitoring processes need to be agreed and implemented. Elearning is 'front loaded' in terms of time, just as **distance learning** is; the need for preparation and planning are crucial to both.

Quality assurance processes are often imposed by bodies external to the university, and compliance can therefore be given grudgingly. However, when staff negotiate their own standards, the quality of elearning programmes is usually higher. Furthermore, compliance is self-sustaining without enforcement or policing.

The problem of **plagiarism** in elearning programmes has an impact on quality. Plagiarism is not a problem unique to elearning, but it is certainly exacerbated by the ease with which material from the **web** can be cut and pasted into an essay and passed off as original work by the student. Furthermore, whole essays can be bought online and websites offering to tailor material for specific essay topics can easily be found. Plagiarism detection **software** has been developed to cope with the problem, and student guidelines have been developed to increase awareness and understanding about plagiarism. Re-designing assessments to tie them in to the online discussions, and to include a succession of drafts or outlines, is more effective and can lead to better quality work from students.

Evaluation of the learning provision by the educational institution is as essential for elearning as it is for face-to-face teaching. Developing web-based questionnaires is the obvious procedure on elearning programmes. As always with programme evaluation measures and processes, it is critical to build these into the programme design from the beginning.

Examples of elearning quality assurance guidelines are those developed by The Quality Assurance Agency of the UK for distance education which are applicable to elearning as well. An Australian framework has also been developed (see **URLs** below). Most higher education institutions have quality assurance processes for learning and if they teach online, these have been adapted or rewritten.

Web links

http://www.qaa.ac.uk/academicinfrastructure/codeofpractice/
distancelearning/default.asp
http://www.aqf.edu.au/quality.htm

RETENTION

This term describes the ability to retain learners over the course of a
module of study, rather than having them drop out as a result of any
difficulties that they might experience. Due to the fact that elearning
enables students to pursue their studies in a solitary environment, rather
isolated from other students, concern has been expressed that often
their problems remain undetected until it is too late and they withdraw
from the course. There is very little hard evidence in the academic
literature that the retention rate for elearners is either better or worse
than other forms of **distance learning**, but where the **motivation** of
elearners is strong, the additional flexibility is frequently perceived as an
advantage. The main problem stems from the fact that in most elearning situations, the learners are at locations remote from the **tutor**, who
is not therefore in a position to spot learner difficulties as s/he might do
in a classroom situation. For this reason, many educationalists have
developed a variety of ways to encourage **interaction** between learners
and to foster participation in **tutor groups** that allow early identification of developing problems. Regular formative **assessment** to give
constructive **feedback** to learners on their academic progress, together
with a range of **online** support resources, (such as tips on how to write
a good essay, how to reference properly etc.) have been used to assist
learners to feel more comfortable with the more individualistic
demands of elearning.

It is common for universities that make significant use of elearning to
allocate a student adviser to each course, with the aim of providing a
level of personal support for students that is not directly linked to the
learner's tutor (and therefore to any learning problems associated with
the teaching style of that tutor).

ROLE PLAY

A form of educational **interaction** and **peer-to-peer** communication
between learners in which the participants take on the role(s) of char-

acters other than themselves. In **games and gaming** this may take the form of an **avatar** as a representation of the participant, who controls the movement of that character in the **online** environment. It has been employed extensively both in online and in offline educational contexts, particularly with reference to **problem–based learning** (**PBL**) and vocational learning/training situations. In elearning it is common to use a **discussion board** and assign roles to students to facilitate a learning activity, e.g. chair a meeting, present an alternative point of view (with supporting evidence), summarise and propose action points, in order to demonstrate that students are fully conversant with a particular subject. A key point is usually that the role is more important than the result of the role-playing, and is used to provide a means for learners to gain experience in playing different roles, e.g. being 'for' or 'against' in a debate, even though the participant may personally hold contrary views.

SCREEN DUMP

Also called a screenshot, this is a copy of the image that is actually on your computer screen. It can either be printed out on paper, or copied as an image and pasted into another document, such as a word-processed file. Although the image resolution of screen dumps may not be sharp, they are frequently used for instructing learners how they should progress through a sequence of tasks. A screen dump can usually be generated by depressing the 'Print Screen' key on a computer keypad and can then be pasted or printed. A screen shot has the advantage that it generates an exact image of what is on your computer screen at that instant, and so is a convenient way of guiding a new student or hesitant learner through a variety of screens or **webpages** that might seem to be quite intimidating. A common way to use screen dumps for instructing students is to direct them to a particular **URL**, then issue them with specific instructions, for example:

'Go to www.uhi.ac.uk; your screen should now look like this.'

Figure 8 Screen dump

Now click on the link to "Academic partners" in the right-hand column and select your choice of academic partner from the list that appears in left-hand column'

Screen dumps can be used to quickly construct a guide to an **online** activity and can be disposed with or updated when the images change. They provide a simple way to ease new learners into navigating the **web** or to **download** an item from the **internet**.

SEARCH ENGINE

A **software** application on the **internet** the main purpose of which is to allow the user to search rapidly through the **web** in order to identify and locate documents relevant to their needs. Usually the learner will be asked to type a number of key search terms into a search box to produce a list of relevant **webpages**. The webpages will often be ranked in order of priority according to appropriate descriptive information (called **metadata**) that is used to catalogue web-based information. Searches can be a straight search by typing relevant key words (such as 'rural health' for items on rural health) but the increasing popularity and extent of the web means that general searches such as this often turn up millions of supposedly relevant webpages. More specific searches can be achieved by the use of the + sign (e.g. 'rural+health+community') or by enclosing the relevant string of characters in quotation marks (e.g. 'Frank Rennie' will search only for this string of alphabetic characters). As with any key word search, choosing the most appropriate term is crucial. For example a search for 'agriculture' will produce a different (though hopefully overlapping) set of webpages than a search for the term 'farming'.

Probably the most popular search engine currently is Google www.google.co.uk but www.kartoo.com and www.bestsearch.com are also popular.

SELF-DIRECTED LEARNING

As with many of the terms used in elearning, there is a range of concepts closely associated if not synonymous with self-directed learning. A list of these terms acts more or less as a definition of self-directed learning:

- **student–centred** learning;
- independent learning;
- developmental learning;
- autonomous learning;
- individualised learning;
- learner-managed learning;
- resource-based learning.

The term self-directed learning came to prominence in the 1970s and 1980s, and has subsequently been somewhat devalued as simply a means of transferring the cost of learning to the learners. With the advent of elearning, however, the term or at least the concept behind it, has become associated with the move away from teacher-directed to student-directed learning. The failure of much **CBT** used without any teacher support, has shown the continuing importance of the teacher, but the teacher in the form of **facilitator**, rather than sage on the stage. Two of the basic premises of self-directed learning are that people need to be empowered to take personal responsibility for their own learning, and that the perceived needs of learners should drive the content and design of the course.

In formal elearning, self-directed learning usually involves activities that the students carry out either individually or collaboratively. These might be problems to solve, a project to complete, a dilemma to resolve or a topic to discuss. The **tutor** is needed to manage the process, comment on student messages, advise and point to resource materials and generally humanise the **online** environment. In some online programmes, especially postgraduate courses, students are given more autonomy: e.g. to participate in establishing the agenda and sometimes even the **assessment**, to make choices about what they will study, to take turns moderating the discussions, to carry out peer and self-assessments, to discover and make use of resources on the **internet**. These are all aspects of self-directed learning.

There are two elements in the establishment of a self-directed learning environment online: the willingness of the student to become self-directed, and the approach of the tutor in passing control to the students. There is evidence of resistance from both students and tutors. With students, the resistance can result from lack of skill, lack of time or lack of interest. Teacher-directed approaches are generally more familiar, easier and less time-consuming. Online collaborative activities are a prime example of self-directed learning in that students are actively involved in constructing knowledge and in creating a positive learning environment. However, they are time-consuming; they do need good team working skills and they can require students to find, analyse and present material from external resources. With online tutors, the resistance is not dissimilar: lecturing is more familiar, facilitating seems to be giving up authority, and in the initial stages, elearning can be more time-consuming than lecturing. Online tutors need to be really interested in their learners; they need to listen to them as individuals and work with them to explore viewpoints and perspectives.

Scaffolding of the process of becoming a self-directed learner is the solution most often proposed to overcome student resistance. The online course should be designed to gradually demand more and more input from the students. The tutor should set out initially to model the desired kind of commenting, questioning and reflecting that students are expected to develop. It is important that the tutor withdraws this level of commenting as the students begin to work on the activities; otherwise, they will continue to 'sit back' and wait for the tutor to comment.

Staff training and online experience are the best antidotes to tutor resistance. The skill of interacting with students online is not something for which lecturing, researching and writing academic papers are a good preparation. Tutors need to develop ways of stimulating in depth, online **interaction**, using their understanding of the subject, their ability to identify significant ideas and question those less relevant, and their knowledge of useful resource materials. What they need to practice is the skill of encouraging students and supporting multiplicity of perspectives, while still pushing them to examine assumptions, beliefs and ideas.

Furthermore, tutors need to be able to do this through the written word and to do it with warmth, enthusiasm and respect for the individual learner.

This move to a student-centred approach is truly a two-way process. Where students have entrenched expectations about the role of the teacher, tutors can be 'compelled' by their students to adopt teacher-centred methods despite their best efforts.

It has been shown that students who have already developed self-direction in their learning – for example, those who view their success as due to their own work, those who welcome choice as an opportunity rather than a threat, those who understand that they can learn from their peers – are most likely to be successful on elearning programmes. Not surprisingly, this type of student is more often found in postgraduates than undergraduates, in the self-confident than the unself-confident, in mature rather than immature learners. It is not a question of age, but rather of learning experience, self-perception and **motivation**. However, there is also research evidence showing that students can develop more self-direction and that elearning is an ideal vehicle for this transformation.

Informal elearning demonstrates many of the characteristics of self-directed learning. Informal learning encompasses the lifelong process of acquiring knowledge, skills, attitudes and insights from, in the case of elearning, browsing online, being a member of one or more online **communities**, buying and selling online, and using the search and **hyperlink** facilities of the **web** to investigate a subject or pursue a hobby. It is the authentic nature of this kind of learning which is most significant. Informal learners take part in these activities because they have a need or a purpose for doing it, and it is their interest and motivation that dictates the amount of time, the subject matter, the focus and their level of participation. Studies show that informal learning accounts for the great bulk of any person's lifetime learning.

Web links

http://www.itdl.org/Journal/Jun_04/article07.htm
http://www-distance.syr.edu/sdlhome.html

SEMANTIC WEB

The Semantic Web extends the current, human-readable **web** by providing a common framework for data to be shared and reused by machines on a global scale. In short, it is a globally linked **database**. Tim

Berners-Lee, inventor of the web is the originator of the Semantic Web concept, though it is a collaborative effort led by the W3C consortia along with many other researchers and industrial partners. Their aim is to improve, extend and standardise existing systems and tools, and to develop languages for expressing information in a form which machines can process. The result should be a web which increases users' ability to find the appropriate information. Using content tags and well defined meanings, the Semantic Web will enable computers to 'understand' what they are displaying and to communicate more effectively with each other.

The problem with the current web is that it returns tens of thousands of results, when only one is wanted. The lack of an efficient means of finding, sorting and classifying information is the problem that the Semantic Web seeks to address. When fully implemented it promises to return fewer results but with more meaning because it is a more efficient way of relating data. The development of XML has made a fundamental contribution to its realisation through providing the foundation on which the problems of representing relationships and meaning can be built.

There is considerable controversy over the viability of the Semantic Web and the possibility of developing a machine-readable web; however, there is general agreement that if successful, it will have a radical effect on the web.

SERVER

A piece of computer **software** that carries out a task on behalf of another piece of software (called a **client**) such as gaining access to **email**, or **webpages**. The term is now in common use to refer to the **hardware**, such as the computer, that runs the software, but this is more accurately referred to as the **web** server. In terms of popular access to the **internet**, a server functions within computer **networks** to provide a host for webpages or software applications that can be remotely accessed by users. In the context of elearning, students will connect with the school/college/university server in order to access the institutional **VLE** or **MLE**, but will most likely be aware of the existence of the server only when it ceases to function due to a technical fault (described as the server being 'down').

SIMULATION

In the context of elearning, a simulation is a learning resource that attempts to model **virtual reality** in order to illustrate a specific educational objective. Commonly a simulation will generate a number of different scenarios in response to the user changing the initial parameters used to categorise the simulation, and may produce an **animation** to illustrate the results of this modelling. A simulation may be used to extend a **case study**, and might include **audio/video clips** and **role play** as well as web-based **graphics** and scenario-building. An advantage of a simulation in education is that it allows the manipulation of data to model outcomes in a relatively risk-free environment, or one in which learners would not normally be allowed access e.g. potentially dangerous laboratory experiments or airline flight training.

SITUATED LEARNING

Among the various theories of learning there is an argument that learning occurs best through social **interaction** as this combines a learning activity embedded within its general cultural background and the specific learning context of the knowledge. Situated learning is in contrast to classroom-based learning that tends to be based upon abstract knowledge with less reference to individual context. It is closely related to **experiential learning** and also to **activity-based learning.** Situated learning is an important facet of elearning in that it puts emphasis on the social interaction between learners as part of learning **communities** (e.g. communities of practice or communities of interest). Some theorists have proposed that situated learning is usually unintentional, rather than deliberate, as the individual learners become more involved in their community and begin to identify common values, interests and beliefs that they share.

Commonly, situated learning is focused upon problem-solving skills, or applied knowledge, and examples in the literature frequently identify situations of **peer-to-peer** learning where novices to the community share information with old-timers to their mutual advantage. The **collaborative work** and skills that are identified in studies of situated learning are similar to the key attributes in the promotion of good elearning, namely encouraging participation in the community, interactive learning activities that test the context of the learning, and clear, easily identifiable learning objectives. Learning activities are typically short and focused (c.f. a **webpage** or **learning objects**) and this may lend itself particularly well to just-in-time learning e.g. by following relevant links via a web **browser** or **portal**. The link with **distributed education** is of key importance in that the learner is able to select from a variety of learning resources and learning styles in order to best suit their own individual context of learning.

Learning theories (including situated learning): http://www.educationau. edu.au/archives/cp/04.htm

SKYPE

A **software** application that makes use of the **voice–over–internet protocol** (VoIP) available to **broadband** users to make high quality audio and video connections with remote contacts. In effect skype allows users to make 'free' telephone calls and/or connect **synchronous** video images between users. Technology such as this has a wider application for business and commercial transactions, but is being incorporated in elearning pedagogy (see **distributed education**) due to the advantages of making learning **interaction** more immediate for remote students. It also provides a level of learner support, with the learner being able to contact the **tutor** or peer group for short conversations at times when help is needed.

SNAIL MAIL

A derogatory term for the conventional post delivery services of letters etc. and used to emphasise the slow speed of delivery of paper-based communications in comparison to the almost instantaneous delivery of **email** or **text messaging**. Despite this, postal delivery of course materials etc. continues to be used as a complement to electronic versions and/or as a backup e.g. a **tutor** may post a CD with course materials as well as making this available on an **MLE** or another **webpage**. The advantages of this are that learners are not entirely dependent upon accessing their learning resources solely via the **internet**, and that they can combine the convenience of both electronic and hard copies.

SOCIAL CAPITAL

This is a hotly debated social science term that is used to describe the collective value of networks of **trust**, mutual understanding and reciprocal help that facilitate coordination and cooperation in **communities** for mutual benefit. In the 1990s some social scientists began to look at the nature of community in a different way. They made the case that the more strongly people identify themselves by their membership of a community, and the more they feel that they have a full role to play in the life and decision-making roles of their community, then the more strongly that group actually functions as a community. It has been suggested that while economic capital resides in people's bank accounts, and human capital is inside their heads, then social capital is vested in the structure of their relationships. People's sense of community is derived from their perception of being linked into a complex system of relationships and **interaction**, and these shared experiences help to foster group solidarity and a sense of common purpose. This is a key advantage in **online** learning communities, where participants rarely know each other, may never meet, and may have little in common apart from their interest in the subject being studied.

By acting together in a common space, members of a community learn from each other to foster a sense of collective identity, which they seek to define and reinforce by constructing 'rules' of behaviour (however rigid or loose) through which they can achieve a general consensus that is consistent with their common interests. The ways by which these norms are constructed, reinforced and enforced will be different between different communities, and this is as true between geographical communities as it is between geographical and 'virtual' communities. Networking is a vital component of community development, and in this respect online communities offer advantages over geographical 'communities of place' because distributed communities are able to overcome the necessity of being in the same location and/or the same time to engage in collective dialogue or decision-making.

A key community-building element resulting from social networking is the fostering of trust between the members of the **network**, partly from sharing stories and partly through being exposed to the stories of participants who seem to be similar to themselves in some ways, but to be different in other ways. The **web** has emerged as a new technological vehicle for harvesting the personal experiences of others and the construction of tools that attempt to make this collective activity more visible (and accessible) is a major research field. Studies show that reciprocal support is a vital part of community networks, both online and in a physical location, though this may manifest itself in a wide range of ways, from baby-sitting, to practical comfort in times of stress, to the praise and celebration of a successful task well done. At the heart of collaborative activity, there is an understanding that participants contribute something positive when they are able to, in the realisation that they may be required to draw on the support of others at some point in the future. Social capital, sometimes referred to as 'the glue that holds a community together', increases a community's productive potential in several ways, by sharing ideas, resources and expertise, by networking information more quickly, and by encouraging **peer-to-peer** learning as well as collective responsibility. This is an important aspect of collaborative learning activities, and the many-to-many **accessibility** of online interactive networks means that 'virtual communities' have profound implications not simply for learning, but for understanding social change in general.

SOFTWARE

Any computer program or set of organised instructions designed to make an electronic device (such as a computer or a printer) perform in a deliberate manner. The software is normally hosted on some physical infrastructure termed the **hardware**, and is purchased separately from the hardware (although retailers are now commonly selling a 'bundle' of hardware plus basic software to new users). Typical software applications include the common computer programs that are used to do word-processing, **database** compilation, or to connect to the **internet** to send **email** or do some **surfing**.

SPAM

Although this term was originally used as a slang expression for the practice of sending an excessive amount of data to a computer system in order to make it crash (cease to function), it has come to mean any unwanted and unsolicited **post** to a **bulletin board** or **email** in-tray. Common spam includes advertisements for various unwanted products or attempts to get recipients to sign up for events and activities that they would normally avoid. Apart from the nuisance value of spam – since every message has to be read, or at least identified, before it can be deleted – the objections to spam are that it slows down network performance by taking up memory space and **bandwidth** with unnecessary (and unwanted) messages. Most **internet service providers** (**ISP**) now include a routine spam filter as part of their service to customers, although of course spammers are constantly inventing new ways to break through the barriers.

STUDENT-CENTRED LEARNING – OR LEARNER-CENTRED LEARNING

An approach to teaching in which the experience of the learner is central. The focus is on how the students are learning, what they experience and how they engage in the learning process. Through a process of gradual empowerment student-centred learning focuses on student outcomes rather than on teaching. While references to student centred learning abound in the literature, definitions are often confused with other teaching strategies. A range of similar terms are:

- **self-directed learning**;
- learner-focused learning;
- autonomous learning;
- independent learning;
- **collaborative** learning;
- **experiential learning**;
- authentic learning;
- **problem-based learning**;
- constructivist learning.

To generalise about all of these terms, it is possible to say that they give students greater autonomy and control over choice of subject matter, learning methods or pace of study. Some student centred approaches concentrate on giving students more input into:

- What is learned;
- How it is learned; or
- When it is learned.

An important implication of this definition is that students need to assume a high level of responsibility in the learning situation and be actively choosing their goals and managing their learning. They can no longer rely on the lecturer to tell them what, how, where and when to think. Many students, in particular surface learners, tend to want to be told what to do and what to think. There is often a feeling among students that the **tutor** has been paid to teach and should set about teaching. The tradition of 'telling as teaching' is strong. How far is one prepared to move from this tradition toward more student centred approaches and risk poor appraisals by students?

Student-centred learning is often contrasted with teacher-centred learning as Figure 9 summarises.

Teacher-centred learning	Student-centred learning
Teacher prescribes learning goals and objectives based on prior experiences, past practices and existing mandated standards.	Students work with teachers to select learning goals and objectives based on authentic problems and students' prior knowledge, interests and experience.
Students expect teachers to teach them what's required to pass the test. Passive recipients of information. Reconstructs knowledge and information.	Teacher provides multiple means of accessing information and acts as facilitator, helps students access and process information.
Teacher organises and presents information to groups of students and acts as gatekeeper of knowledge, controlling students' access to information.	Students take responsibility for learning. Active knowledge seekers. Construct knowledge and meaning.
Assessment used to sort students. Exams used to assess students' acquisition of information. Teacher sets performance criteria for students.	Assessment is an integral part of learning. Performance-based, used to assess students' ability to apply knowledge. Students develop self-assessment and peer assessment skills.
Teachers serve as the centre of epistemological knowledge, directing the learning process and controlling student's access to information. Students viewed as 'empty' vessels and learning is viewed as an additive process. Instruction is geared for the 'average' student and everyone is forced to progress at the same rate.	Learning is an active dynamic process in which connections are constantly changing and their structure is continually reformatted. Students construct their own meaning by talking, listening, writing, reading, and reflecting on content, ideas, issues and concerns.

Figure 9 Contrast of teacher-centred and student-centred learning

Further reading

Dane J. 'Designing Environments that Stimulate Student-Centred Learning' at www.temchobart2004.com/downloads/31_DANE.doc

SURFING

The procedure of navigating over the **web** using a **search engine** to display and select **webpages** that are of interest to the user. Surfing is sometimes also called 'browsing' due to the fact that **software** called a web **browser** is used to connect the user's computer with the search engine and then display the results.

SYNCHRONOUS LEARNING

Learning activities are synchronous when they allow learners to have a level of **interactivity** at the same moment of time, e.g. a **face-to-face** (**f2f**) meeting, a live **videoconference**, a telephone conversation or an **audioconference** discussion. Due to the fact that elearning and **distributed education** in general allow for a wide diversity of **asynchronous learning** activities, it is usual to qualify whether a 'meeting' of learners (and **tutors**) is planned to occur synchronously or asynchronously. It is common to refer to a mix of synchronous and asynchronous learning activities (e.g. **online learning** plus face-to-face lectures) as **blended learning**, although there is a blurring of the boundaries with distributed education.

TEXT MESSAGING

Although this can be applied to any textual form of communication, such as **email**, it is generally now only applied to short message service (SMS) messages via mobile phones. Also called 'texting' or txt, there are currently relatively few applications specifically for elearning due largely to the reliance on a small hand-held screen. Text messaging has enjoyed a phenomenal growth over the past few years, especially among young people, and some student services facilities have sought to capitalise upon this, e.g. by sending library notifications or overdue notices by text messaging to students' mobile phones.

THREADED DISCUSSION

A threaded discussion is a series of messages on a particular topic **posted** in a **discussion board** forum. These discussions are **asynchronous** and the conversations occur amongst a group of learners. 'Threads' allow the reader to follow the various contributions to the discussion and respond to specific messages. A running log is thus created of remarks and opinions which build up over time. Users email their comments, and the computer maintains them in order of originating message then replies to that message. The educational applications are:

- Good for supporting thoughtful responses where reflection is warranted;
- Appropriate where **face-to-face (f2f)** opportunities are limited or impossible;
- Easy to integrate with other **online** or offline activities;
- Can be particularly useful with quiet or reflective learners who might not participate in a classroom discussion.

Successful educational discussions usually require careful guidance and structure from the instructor. Examples of useful approaches include: providing timelines for the discussion, some form of accountability, specific tasks or roles for each participant. Debates are one useful structure; student presentations are another. Although the teacher provides the overall guidance, it is important that students feel they control the **interaction** and have the opportunity to develop their own understanding of the issues. Offering students the chance to moderate the discussion for a period can be a good way of giving students just this opportunity.

Part of the educational benefit of this kind of discussion is the exposure students get to different perspectives and varying interpretations by reading the various threads. There is research evidence that the asynchronous nature of threaded discussion offers valuable time for reflection, which can in turn lead to higher order thinking: exploring, integrating and resolving issues. There is disagreement about whether it is advisable to award students marks for the nature or number of postings. On the one hand, it encourages participation; on the other, it can lead to students writing for the teacher.

Threaded discussions are used in chat rooms on the **internet** and on **online** services as well as in groupware products.

TMA

A Tutor Marked Assignment is a piece of work submitted to a course **tutor** by a learner for marking as part of a structured learning experience. Normally the learner will get some **feedback** from the tutor, as well as a mark or grade that can be used to assess their performance and/ or understanding of the course. A TMA can range very widely in style to cover essays, reports, book reviews, individual or group projects, presentations and a variety of other form of measuring learners' levels of understanding. Diversity in the type of TMA can support the different needs of learners, and links positively with the diversity of resources available in **distributed education**. Contrasts with **CMA**.

TOOLBAR

This is usually a row or column of **icons** that are displayed at the top, bottom, or side of a computer screen to allow quick and easy navigation to other **software** (such as another office application), tasks (such as printing or saving) or other locations (such as a folder or an additional drive). The toolbar can usually be customised to appear on the **desktop** when the user decides to **logon**, and often the choice of icons or task buttons can be selected by the user to display a palette of the user's most common tasks or software applications. Individual software applications may have their own toolbars to allow easy navigation when using this application.

TROJAN

This is a type of computer **virus** that is designed to be deliberately destructive to computer files and/or their operating systems. It was initially named after the 'Trojan horse' of Greek mythology due to the fact that the virus was concealed within other files that masqueraded as **games** or pieces of useful information. Unlike a **worm**, the Trojan is specifically created to cause damage to the users of computer **networks**, but a good, modern, virus protection **software** hosted by most reputable **ISPs** should be sufficient safeguard for most users.

TRUST

A key element in the construction of online **communities** resulting from social networking is the fostering of trust between the members of the **network**. Learning activities that encourage learner interaction, through **discussion boards**, or collaborative activities, can also stimulate the development of trust, and this is important in several ways. In the first instance learners are encouraged to participate more fully when they have a measure of trust in their fellow participants, e.g. that their contributions to the discussion will be valued and not be ridiculed. Second, trust is important for the establishment of **peer-to-peer** learning whereby learners can share experiences and come to regard each other as trusted sources of knowledge. Two components are key to the formation of this trust: reliability and reciprocity. Obviously it is important that shared information is reliable and can contribute towards the learning experience, and in this context trust can be accumulated in a participant who consistently supplies accurate information, or lost by the supply of less reliable contributions. It is interesting to note that some **online** auction facilities, such as eBay, award a rating to participants based upon **feedback** on the quality of their services, reliability, promptness and so on. In terms of reciprocity, if the participants in group-learning activities feel in some way that their help to others might be returned at some point in the future, this can act as a powerful bonding force in the group.

Trust also has wider connotations, for example, that information divulged online will not be misused, or that apparently valuable sources of information such as a useful **website**, a specialist **portal** giving access to themed information sources, or reports provided by individual **blogging** enthusiasts are in fact what they claim to be. The **web** has emerged as a new technological vehicle for harvesting the personal experiences of others and the construction of tools that attempt to make this collective activity more visible (and accessible) is a major research field.

TUTOR GROUP

A group of students assigned to a particular **tutor** who guides them through an **internet** learning experience. The primary role of the tutor is to develop a rapport with the students and add a human touch to the process of learning. Responsibilities of the tutor vary but usually involve encouraging discussions, exploring ideas and commenting on students' messages. Students in the group may work collaboratively and may be asked to take leadership roles, such as leading a discussion, in order to develop **online** skills. **Interaction** can be through **discussion boards, chatrooms, email, audioconferencing** or text and **webpages**. Communication can be one-to-one with the tutor or another student, or one-to-many with the whole tutor group.

Many students form close attachments with the other students in the tutor group through sharing problems, solutions and resources. **Online** tutors need to prioritise their workload, as students can be overly demanding. Their key aim is to build student confidence and develop their understanding of the material.

The success of the tutor group as a learning environment is partially dependent on the input of the tutor and partially on the design of the course. The attitude of the tutor is evident in the extent to which:

- they value and encourage students' ideas and questions;
- they see students as partners in a learning journey;
- they share their field of expertise;
- they actively search for ways to help students learn.

The design of the course also has an impact on the working of the tutor group:

- Learning activities – opportunities are generated for students to explore their own hypotheses, promoting scholarly and reflective practices consistent with skill development as lifelong learners;
- **Assessment** – methods are designed to be fair and give opportunities for different kinds of learners to show what they know;
- Support materials – formal communications (subject guides, learning outcomes and assessment guidelines, timetables etc.) are clear, specific and in writing.

TUTORING

Tutoring **online**, or e-moderating as it is sometimes called, involves the support, management and **assessment** of students in an elearning environment. It is generally accepted that the effort and skill of the **tutor** are the key to successful **online** learning. In some cases the tutor is also the instructor who develops the course or programme, usually from a **face-to-face** (**f2f**) mode to the online mode, or to a **blended** mode. In other cases, the content and **web** development are carried out by a team of people, each expert in different aspects of the process e.g. web design, pedagogy and administration.

Tutoring online primarily requires a change of attitude from lecturing face-to-face, in that the tutor is not in control of the situation to the same extent as the lecturer in front of a class. The tutor's role is much closer to that of a **facilitator**, supporting students, guiding them to resources, advising about assignments and managing the online environment. The latter might involve setting up new discussion areas as required, keeping track of student progress and assessment results, or initiating collaborative activities. In some contexts, the tutor may be expected to use **video-conferencing** or **audioconferencing**, communicate one-to-one with students by telephone. The main task of the tutor, however, is to be the subject expert, summarising discussion topics, correcting misunderstandings and marking assignments. Social skills are more important online than they are in face-to-face teaching. Tutors need to be engaging, reassuring, welcoming and supporting. They also need to make sure that the online discussion areas are not dominated by one or two students, and that shy and unconfident students are encouraged to participate.

There are many courses offered online in how to tutor. However, the most valuable learning is through practice and experience of the online environment. Taking an online course and experiencing the process of being an online student can be a good way of developing a sensitivity for online learning. Just as students need to become comfortable interacting online, perhaps with people they never meet, so the tutor needs to establish an individual tutoring style that feels comfortable. Many teaching skills are as applicable online as face-to-face e.g. ability to explain topics clearly and to provide useful **feedback** to students on their assignments, and enthusiasm for the subject area. Additional skills needed to teach online are: willingness to engage with students in their learning process, ability to facilitate group discussions and flexibility in responding to the unpredictability of the medium. The online environment has strengths and weaknesses, and the tutor needs to be aware of these and find ways of maximising the benefits and minimising the limitations of the medium.

Online tutors, like elearners, need to develop their understanding of what the **web** can offer and their ability to find and assess the value of web resources. The web may be the richest, most varied and easily accessed information source that has ever been available, but developing the skill to discriminate between a good website and a poor one is something that tutors and elearners both need to address. Amongst other things, they need to consider the accuracy and depth of information, visual attractiveness and relevance to the course.

There are a number of crucial tasks for the tutor to perform at the beginning of an online course:

1. It is important for tutors to make clear what their students can expect from them e.g. how often and when they will **log on**, what level of support they will provide and where to put their technical queries.
2. An **email** message from the tutor to each student at the beginning or even before the start of the course is highly recommended. This might contain an introduction to the course, any essential administrative information and some background about the tutor, but most important is the reassuring tone established by the message. Although most of the content will be the same for each learner, it is ideal if the tutor sends this initial message to each student individually, addressing them by name and perhaps noting any details about the student gained from the registration information.
3. Tutors should devote more time to online **interaction** in the initial

phase of the course than at any subsequent phase. For example, as each student enters the **discussion board** area, tutors should make sure that a response is made either by another student or by making one themselves. Students feel particularly vulnerable about communicating 'in public' at the beginning of a course, and need encouragement and reassurance that they are on the right track. Likewise it is important at the beginning of the course that tutors answer any email promptly. If the learner poses a question that cannot be answered quickly then the tutor should send a holding reply, acknowledging receipt of the email and explaining that they will answer as soon as possible, ideally giving some indication of when that will be.

4. Messages arising from the early activities also need more comments from the tutor until the process of peer commenting is established. In the first phase of the course, the tutor is modelling this skill of giving feedback. Comments should be positive yet honest and challenging. This is part of the process of developing **trust** which is an essential component of online **community**.

The skill of the online tutor is in developing a way of responding to online discussions that is constructive and encouraging, but also that challenges the learners by asking relevant questions that will move the group forward in their learning. This questioning approach must be conducted with tact and care. It must neither seem like an interrogation nor a list of set questions that are not tailored to the group. Too many questions can be overwhelming and students rarely answer any of them. One or two questions per message are enough. It is often useful if the tutor provides some indication of how a question could be answered or gives a personal view or opinion. This allows the learners a hook on which to hang their response.

Web links

http://users.sa.chariot.net.au/~michaelc/nw2001/emod_newlang.htm
http://www.nettskolen.com/forskning/20/moderating.html

UPLOAD

The transfer of data from one computer onto another computer or **network**. This term is often confused with the term **download**. A common occurrence for elearners is the need to upload their **TMA** or other pieces of pre-prepared text onto a **discussion board** or some other section of an **MLE**. Normally this is achieved simply by sending an **email** to the relevant site and adding the TMA as an **attachment**. The ability to upload data is similar to the constraints on downloading, i.e. small, simple files are transferred quickly and easily, but larger, more complex files often require **broadband** to function efficiently. Usually the **internet** connection is **asynchronous** in its **bandwidth**, with the property of being able to download data at a faster rate than it is possible to upload the same data. This is due to the fact that the network is designed to **surf** the **web** and receive data, rather than send out large volumes of data from a domestic computer.

URL

Commonly also called 'web addresses', the Uniform Resource Locator is a standardised address for **web** resources that both identifies the resource and tells how to find it. In many ways a URL is the basic building block of the web as far as individual users are concerned as it specifies the specific location of each individual resource on the web in a generic format that is unique to that particular resource, but can also be extended to include other similar resources. An example of this might indicate an article stored as a document or a **pdf** file, in a certain folder, on a particular **server**, hosted by a named organisation, in a certain country. The URL for my **homepage** within my institution is at the following address: http://www.lews.uhi.ac.uk/about/research/ StaffRec1.htm.

VALIDATION

This is a general term that refers to the **quality assurance** process for approving a degree or similar academic award. The validation process will normally consist of a thorough testing of all aspects of the award, including **course design**, appropriate resources, methods of delivery and **assessment**, staff expertise and the contents/context of the learning materials. This would include access to any **online libraries** and **MLE** that would be available to the prospective learners. The scrutiny may or may not be conducted by specialists who are external to the awarding-giving body, in collaboration with the normal quality assurance process of the institution. Normally the validation process for online components of an award will be incorporated with and seamless with the approval of 'non–online' components, but an unfamiliarity with the theory and practice of **elearning** may sometimes result in the validation panel applying a more rigid quality assurance standard than would be expected for **face–to–face** (**f2f**) delivery.

VIDEOCONFERENCING

As elearning has shifted its interpretation into electronic media other than simply **email** interacting with a set of **web** resources, it has come to include videoconferencing as part of the array of **online** resources. At its simplest, this has been described as a method of conferencing between two or more locations where both sound and vision are conveyed electronically so as to enable simultaneous interactive communication. It is possible to use the **internet** to connect videoconference sites, but due to technical restrictions on data transfer many institutions prefer to use an Integrated Services Digital Network (ISDN) that provides high-quality data transmission in real-time through normal dial–up connections (i.e. without the need for expensive dedicated lines). It is not a new technology, but improvements in equipment, dramatic lowering of the operational costs and the increasing availability of dial–up connections has produced a rapid growth in its use. Multinational companies have been using elements of videoconferencing since the 1960s but it is really only since the mid–1990s that there has been other than experimental use by educational establishments. Essentially there are four main uses of videoconferencing in education:

1. Meetings. Bringing together peers that are distributed over a wide geographical area for whom **face–to–face** (**f2f**) meetings would be costly or prohibitive. This would include supervision meetings with research students located on a campus remote from their supervisor, and also video counseling for remote students. There has been an upsurge of videoconferencing for meetings in the aftermath of September 11 as it is perceived to allow the benefits of visual communication without the necessity of air travel.
2. Teaching. The etiquette of small-group teaching has much in common with the requirements of videoconferencing and has proved a very popular medium for reaching students who are scattered on distributed sites. Initial use simply to replicate a face-to-face lecture has been recognized as counterproductive and this has resulted in a more strategic approach to the use of videoconferencing for teaching. The network communications enable a specialist **tutor** to contribute from a

location other than that of the students (another college, a hospital or laboratory) and this has proved popular with multi-campus universities. It is useful for occasional short presentations by an international specialist to add variety and/or costly detail to a course. It has the additional advantage over **audioconferencing** that it can display a range of visual resources such as Powerpoint slides, documents via overhead camera, as well as the emotional reactions of students.

3. Management. Course committees and other educational bureaucracy can be effectively conducted via videoconference, especially where multi-campus institutions would otherwise incur significant travel costs. The conduct of videoconference meetings requires some additional social considerations to be most effective (see **netiquette**).

4. Interviews. Using **videoconferencing** for interviewing has extended the reach beyond simply **face-to-face** interviews, particularly when considering international applicants for research positions or faculty posts where cost is a consideration.

The main advantages of videoconferencing lie in the ability to link one-to-one or multi-point connections for short, intense contacts that would otherwise be prohibitively expensive to facilitate. It can also be a rich source of learning content, particularly when combined with other learning resources. Disadvantages are that the costs of high-quality equipment still restricts its use to key locations, and that poorer quality connections may result in jerky movements and a time-lag in audio transmission, creating a learning environment that is less spontaneous than face-to-face meetings. Experience shows that videoconference sessions work better between people who have met before, even briefly, and for focused tasks. As a result, the use of videoconference sessions seems to work best intermittently and in combination with other **blended learning** resources for participants who are geographically distributed. This entails bringing participants together synchronously for strategically focused learning events rather than as a standard replacement for lecture presentations.

Web links

http://www.video.ja.net/intro

VIRTUAL REALITY

An effect using computer **software** to create a **simulation** of reality. Although initially created as an environment of total immersion, and speedily adopted for use in **games and gaming**, there has been comparatively little widespread adoption of the technology. Best known examples would include various types of flight simulator programs that give the feeling of actually flying an aircraft, or programs for constructing buildings in 3D that allow users to navigate through the rooms, and are used by the emergency services and military for practicing rescue techniques. With the proliferation of the **web**, an element of virtual reality is sometimes included on **webpages** to give the impression of 3D **graphics** on the 2D computer screen. With the wider availability of **broadband** there is increasing interest in elearning to exploit virtual reality techniques to create educational simulations such as 'virtual field trips' that allow learners to 'visit' features such as landscapes, geological sites, laboratories, or nuclear reactors that would be difficult or impossible for the student to visit in real life.

VIRTUAL SEMINAR

Sometimes also called a **webinar**, this is an **online** form of academic seminar that is extended over a specified period of time, perhaps 1–3 days, to provide an **asynchronous learning** experience over the **web**. Normally a virtual seminar is dedicated to a specific topic of study and is conducted through a **discussion board** on a **VLE** with a small group of more advanced learners. Commonly a presentation is given, or a piece of set reading to which learners are asked to respond and actively challenge. Key elements of a virtual seminar are that the learning experience encourages **interaction**, that **peer-to-peer** learning is supported, and that the activity is **online**, facilitated by **ICT**. In contrast to a **webcast**, which is one-directional, a webinar promotes and supports multiple connections, including in some cases **email** messages and **audioconference** links with the virtual seminar site, which may later be translated into **text messages** on the discussion board. Some use the term 'virtual seminar' to include seminars conducted by **videoconference**, but though the boundaries may be blurred, the term webinar explicitly requires the use of web-based **software** applications for participation.

VIRTUAL UNIVERSITY

This concept rose to prominence in the 1990s as a means of offering students maximum flexibility, independence and in some instances individual services. The term denotes a university that uses predominantly virtual learning processes as well as examination and administrative services. In some cases the virtual university is a consortium of participating institutions. A range of **synchronous** and **asynchronous** communication technologies are an integral feature of most such universities. Communication amongst the students and faculty is a central feature of the learning process, though in some instances the teaching method is self-study of course materials. **Online library** resources and teaching material which could consist of **animations, simulations,** video clips or **learning objects** are the other main components of the virtual offering. Some virtual teaching is by video lectures, accessed by the students either synchronously or asynchronously.

Peer learning and collaborative activities, **online** seminars and presentations, guest lectures and **webcasts** are the main teaching methods.

Online registration for new and returning students is usually supported, as is course choice and access to personal information, academic results and financial status. Some virtual universities have also implemented online payment, so that the student never has to come to the university. The wave of enthusiasm for virtual universities has now largely dissipated and although there are still institutions using the word 'virtual' in their title, and even new institutions being proposed, research evidence combined with practical experience favours **blended** approaches. Furthermore, the once-separate models of distance and on-campus teaching are converging with the applications of **ICT** so that educational functions such as programme and course development, delivery to students, provision of learner support and administration are at most universities a blend of virtual and place-based procedures. Virtual universities have found a niche in the education system: for specialist areas, for post-graduates and work-related degrees, for very small countries or small universities to band together to seek economies of scale.

VIRUS

A computer program that has the ability to replicate itself, spread through computer **networks** (usually attached to **email**) and affect the host computer in a particular manner. The rising popularity of the **internet** produces ideal conditions for a virus to multiply and spread from computer to computer, and though some, such as a **Trojan**, are created to cause deliberate damage, many viruses, such as a **worm**, are written to generate **spam** and/or cause a nuisance to individual computer users. Many viruses are created simply to spread panic and anxiety about security issues among less-informed computer users, and many virus 'scares' are simply **hoaxes**.

Increasingly sophisticated anti-virus **software** provided by **ISP** companies can scan and block many suspect communications, but of course the perpetrators creating viruses have responded by seeking new ways to circumvent anti-virus software. Although viruses are usually quite mild in their effect, and are not intrinsically damaging in themselves, the cumulative damage that they can cause through overstressing **servers**, filling memory space, and time-wasting at work means that the transmission of viruses result in millions of pounds worth of losses to businesses worldwide. Most educational institutes combine a system **firewall**, together with anti-virus scanning software and **password** protection to their **VLE** or **MLE** in order to provide maximum security and comfort for elearners.

VLE

This is an abbreviation for Virtual Learning Environment, meaning the mix of **hardware** and **software** that is used to create **online** learning opportunities outwith the classroom situation. The term originated in a similar context to **virtual reality** constructions, in which educationalists attempted to create a learning environment where learners engaged with learning resources and **tutors** in a manner that was markedly different to the conventional classroom or lecture hall, yet which seemed to contain familiar educational components. In this manner:

- Conventional lecture notes might become **webpages** of short, structured guides to educational topics, with **hyperlinks** to take learners to additional resources;
- Course handouts might be **digitized** and added to the VLE as back-up documents for further reading;
- Tests and formative **assessments** can be shared among all learners, regardless of their geographical locality;
- A **discussion board** might be used to promote **interactive** dialogue between students and staff in a similar manner to an extended classroom conversation;
- Learners have the ability to exchange information in small **tutorial groups** and/or individually by **email** or by **instant messaging** facilities that help to reduce the feeling of working alone.

In short, the VLE attempts to emulate all aspects of the students' learning environment, but in an online manner using **ICT** and, normally, a computer **network** such as the **internet** or a college/university **intranet**.

A number of commercial VLEs are available for purchase (e.g. **Blackboard** or **WebCT**) as well as a growing number of **open source** solutions. Although the term 'VLE' is still frequently used for convenience, as the VLE become more sophisticated and 'user friendly' there has been a tendency to resist the term *virtual* learning environment on the grounds that a *real* learning environment has been created, though it differs markedly from what has been considered as conventional education, i.e. **face-to-face** (**f2f**) education in a classroom or lecture theatre. This has lead to the more popular use of the term Managed Learning Environment (**MLE**) that combines all of the elements of a good VLE, with the addition of organisational management **software** tools such as access to the university's Student Information System, email, secure intranet, **online library** facilities and other educational management facilities that are not directly related to the activities of teaching and learning.

VOICE-OVER-INTERNET PROTOCOL (VoIP)

A **software** agreement that allows users with a **broadband** connection to the **internet** to make telephone calls through their computer. As the user is normally paying for the broadband connection anyway, these calls are essentially free to any other user in the world with the appropriate software, and can connect with conventional telephones for a small additional charge.

WEB

A shortened version of the term World Wide Web, that refers to the enormous, interlinked collection of files, or 'documents' that are made available to people over the **internet**. These **webpages** are easy to create with appropriate **software**, and can contain a huge range of information in the form of text, **graphics** and video or audio files. Webpages are connected via **hyperlinks** that enable users to 'jump' from one page to another, following the users' interests, an activity known as **surfing**. The contents of the web can be scrutinised by using a **search engine** to look for key words in the users' area of interest, producing a list of sites from which the most appropriate webpages can be selected to view. The 'address' of a page on the web is referred to as its **URL**.

WEB-BASED LEARNING

Another synonym for elearning or **online** learning. Course content is easily delivered on the **web** and discussion forums via **email, video-conferencing, discussion boards** and live lectures (videostreaming) are all possible. One of the values of using the web to access course materials is that **webpages** may contain **hyperlinks** to other parts of the web, thus enabling access to a vast amount of web-based information.

Most web-based courses use a virtual learning environment (**VLE**) or managed learning environment (**MLE**), as these combine the functions of discussions, real-time **chatrooms**, online **assessment**, tracking of students' use of the web, course administration as well as course content. Several approaches can be used to develop and deliver web-based learning. At one end is 'pure' distance learning (in which course material, assessment and support is all delivered online, with no **face-to-face (f2f)** contact between students and teachers). At the other end is an organisational **intranet**, which replicates printed course materials online to support what is essentially a traditional face-to-face course. The latter is usually referred to as **blended learning**.

Features of a typical web-based course are:

- teaching material including links to related information and articles e.g. online **databases**, journals, library;
- course information, timetable, course guide;
- formative and summative assessments;
- student management tools (records, statistics, student tracking);
- discussion areas, email and real-time chat facilities.

WEB ENABLED

This is a technical term indicating that an object (or in some cases an organisation) is able to interact with the World Wide **Web** over the **internet**, frequently, but not always, over a **wireless network**. Celebrated examples of web enabled artefacts include statues, paintings and museum exhibits that also have a **web presence** that gives more detailed information, interpretation etc. on the work of art. Some examples of smart textiles and smart clothing have been developed in pursuit of **virtual reality** that allows the user to interact with their environment and/or to simulate real-life conditions in unusual situations e.g. giving the illusion of close proximity between collaborators remote from each other. Web enabled objects have been proposed as useful learning resources that will extend the notion of ubiquitous learning and opportunities for mobile learning i.e. structured learning opportunities while using a laptop computer/ Personal Digital Assistant/ mobile phone while the user is on the move. So far, except for a few well-publicised examples and prototypes, there appears to have been little breakthrough of web enabled objects into elearning, though various opportunities have been forecast in the work of Rheingold and others http://www.rheingold.com/index.html.

WEB PRESENCE

This is the concept that a company, or an individual, has a 'place' on the **web** that can be accessed over the **internet**. Usually this means a **web-page** that is advertised by a web address (or **URL**) such as http://www.routledge.co.uk and this page is used to project an image of the company or individual. The web presence of an organisation may range from a very basic **Welcome page** that simply advertises the organisation and lists their phone number, **email** etc. to a more complex **Homepage** that also provides a variety of **hyperlinks** to other resources and pages on the World Wide Web. The more sophisticated examples of web presence allow users to interact with the website, perhaps to purchase goods or interrogate a **database**, and often provide very useful **feed-back** to the site owner. In terms of elearning, some types of **VLE** incorporate individual web pages for students to **post** their own information, photograph etc., or may link with an individual **weblog** for students to express their own views through journal-type entries **online**.

WEBCAM

A small camera device that connects to your computer and allows video images to be transferred over the **internet** to appear as **webpages** or enable interactivity between remote users through a type of **video-conference** facility on the computer **desktop**. There are two common applications, first to enable remote visual as well as audio **interaction** between users using **software** such as **Netmeeting** or video **Skype**, which usually requires users to have a wide **bandwidth** (e.g. **broad-band**). Second, webcams are used to make a particular view (e.g. a landscape or a room in a building) permanently available via a **hyper-link** on a webpage. In the latter example some links may provide a live video image, but it is also common to transmit a still image of the scene and update this image at a regular interval of time, say every 10 minutes. The use of a webcam is becoming more common in elearning as a means of providing a richer and more intimate connection with learners who are studying at a location remote from their **tutor**.

View from a webcam

http://www.visit-fortwilliam.co.uk/webcam
http://www.lochness.co.uk/livecam

WEBCAST

Webcasting or netcasting refers to the streaming of audio and sometimes video over the **web**. It can also be called **internet** radio. A webcast service makes it possible to broadcast lectures, panel discussions and other events across the campus **network** and the internet. The broadcast can be live or delayed audio and/or video. For example, a university could offer **online** courses consisting of webcast lectures by the instructor or guest lecturer. Students need the appropriate **multimedia** application (for example, RealAudio) in order to view or hear the webcast. This process is referred to as push technology i.e. pushing web-based information to an internet user. Webcast **software** synchronises video, audio and slides.

The term 'streaming' is very similar to webcasting and they are used interchangeably. Technically, webcasting covers all the steps in producing an online broadcast – from capture and coding of content through to delivery, whereas streaming refers to the software that actually delivers the webcast to the user's **desktop** player program over the web. The word streaming comes from the way it works: webcast data is viewed, but not actually downloaded in full and stored on the user's computer – it just streams through in real time, piece by piece.

There are numerous educational benefits of webcasting and the fact that the material can be viewed live as well as stored for later use adds to the range of applications. Live broadcasts have a buzz and motivating effect for many learners, while an archive of webcasts can be reviewed, studied and made available to students for exam preparation. A course consisting primarily of webcasts is not ideal as it is hard to maintain concentration and interest in information coming from a small screen over an extended period of time. As a means of accessing a lecture from a remote expert, or to catch up on a missed lecture, or to review complex information it can be a valuable resource.

WebCT

This is a commercial **VLE** (or, more strictly, **MLE**) that is used by many educational institutions to provide and manage student access to their **online** educational resources. Through the adoption of user-friendly management tools and screen **icons** to identify resources, **tutors** are able to provide **asynchronous** access to their courses and associated online learning materials. In common with other commercially managed learning environments, the software is designed so that, once set up, individual tutors can add and alter the contents of their online courses without any specialised **ICT** knowledge or support. Other popular MLEs include **Blackboard** as well as **open source** environments such as customised variants of Boddington and Moodle.

WEBINAR

A name sometimes used to refer to a **virtual seminar**, or **online** seminar, included as part of a programme of **distributed education**.

WEBLOG *see* blogging

WEBPAGE

As it suggests, this is a 'page' on the World Wide **Web**, usually written in **HTML** script with **hypertext** links to other pages to create a series of linked pages. A number of webpages linked together in a folder on the one computer is often called a website and these are available over the **internet** when read in connection with a **web browser** or a **search engine**. The initial root location is usually referred to as the **homepage**, with subsequent links creating a large connected document, or a specialist **portal** linking to other webpages. A simple webpage lists relevant information, typically in short sentences or paragraphs in order that the user does not need to scroll down too far to read detailed information. Additional information is then linked to related pages that can be 'layered' to give the user access to more detailed information, definitions, examples etc. when required by clicking a link. One advantage of this approach is that it does not overload the user, and allows them to self-select what they want to read or avoid (e.g. not to open large files, complex **graphics** or **audio clips**). More complex webpages contain a number of frames that can be scrolled down and searched independently or used as an easily accessible index for the website. Ideally webpages should be designed for efficient use with a range of different web browsers, a feature that is not always observed in some of the more complex webpages.

WebQuests

These are activities, using **internet** and other resources, which encourage students to use higher order thinking skills. A WebQuest is an inquiry-oriented activity in which most or all of the information used by learners is drawn from the **web**. WebQuests are designed to use learners' time well, to focus on using information rather than looking for it, and to support learners' thinking at the levels of analysis, synthesis and evaluation. WebQuests are effectively higher order learning tools. WebQuests can be combined with **blogs** and **Wikis**.

Further details and examples at: http://webquest.sdsu.edu/

WELCOME PAGE

The opening screen of a **webpage** of an individual or business who has a **web presence**. The welcome page is usually also the **homepage**, though frequently welcome pages are only short, single pages, with very few additional **hyperlinks** or additional webpages. A typical welcome page might have a photograph or other graphic, together with an advertising statement and a list of further contacts, including phone and fax numbers, **email** address and so on. When the welcome page is also the homepage there will be additional links to other information on the organisation or individual and the welcome page may be used as a base to direct the user to other **online** resources.

WIKI

A Wiki (or to use its full name, WikiWikiWeb) is group communication **software** that allows users to create and edit **webpages** very quickly using any **browser**. In fact, 'wiki wiki' means quick in Hawaiian. The notion of 'open editing' is what distinguishes Wikis from so much other **online** groupware. It would seem to be a recipe for chaos and yet users all claim that chaos rarely results and if it does, there are recovery mechanisms. This ethic at the heart of the Wiki is 'soft security', that is, it relies on the **communities**, rather than technology, to enforce order. Furthermore, the Wiki concept encourages democratic use and promotes content composition by non-technical users.

Another defining feature of Wikis is that the content is not 'owned' in the same way as conference messages. Anonymity is not required but it is common, as a page will usually have multiple authors. The essence is group creation and refinement.

Related to open editing and group ownership is the notion of flux: links are added in and out of the page; chronology does not determine the organisation, rather the context does. A Wiki grows through accretions and links, and is constantly changing.

No programming or **HTML** knowledge is required to build a site, edit pages or create **hyperlinks** and crosslinks. Often one person or a small group of users emerge as the primary housekeeper to tidy the site and maintain a logical structure.

Unlike traditional groupware which relies on strict workflows, access restrictions and formal structures, Wikis rely on the group to make up the processes as they go along. This often leads to a very strong sense of community and group identity. As with other online communities, Wikis are a reflection of the care and attention of the users. The most obvious application of a Wiki in education is to develop writing expertise and to write joint documents. The features of the technology which support this are:

- they are fun to use;
- they are easy to use;
- they facilitate revision and refinement;
- they focus on the writing process, not the product.

Some instructors welcome the opportunity for students to develop **network** literacy in which writing for the professor is replaced by group writing in an open, collaborative environment. Wikis are also an ideal tool for group editing of documents.

WIRELESS NETWORK

In general terms this is any **network** that operates without cables and relies on radio communication to carry a signal. Wireless networks may support a variety of devices, including telephones, computers and personal digital assistants, usually to give users access to the **internet** or a

LAN such as an organisational **intranet**. A wireless network may cover a single room, a building, or a wider geographical area. The advantage of a wireless connection to the internet is that it potentially allows users to go **online** from anywhere, not simply at a designated campus or **learning centre**. A wireless **broadband** connection offers the learner the possibility of accessing information such as a **database** or a **VLE** in the pursuit of field-based activities, and therefore extends the boundaries of the learning environment even further outside the conventional classroom. In practice the current coverage of wireless broadband connections is geographically quite limited, and places practical restrictions on the flexibility of wireless network access.

WORM

A particular type of computer **virus** that spreads by replicating itself through computer **networks** connected to the **internet**, especially by attaching themselves to **email**. Most worms do not cause real damage to a computer, unlike a **Trojan**, but they have a nuisance value similar to **spam** and waste valuable **bandwidth**. Although a good virus protection **software** hosted on a reputable **ISP** will offer a measure of protection, the ability of a worm to enter a computer connected to the internet and then send out replicas of itself to all the email addresses contained on that computer, means that worms can easily be spread by users opening an email that has apparently come from a friend. The receipt of a worm is not as serious as receiving a virus, but most advice suggests that users do not open email with any suspect **attachment**.

RECOMMENDED READING

We have chosen ten readings which we recommend as representative of the main issues or sectors in elearning. We have excluded any materials which were not easily available, and have made a point of choosing a number of readings which are freely available online. Five of them are books, of which two are single authored, and three are edited collections, as well as five journal articles. We have also tried to represent the range of literature published in English – in Asia, North America and Europe.

Selwyn, N., Gorrard, S. and Furlong, J. (2006). *Adult Learning in the Digital Age.* **London: Routledge Taylor & Francis Group.**

The research at the core of the book's findings was carried out in Wales and the west of England using questionnaires sent to over 1,000 adults and interviews with 100 respondents to the survey. The aim of the researchers was to examine the rhetoric propounded by governments about the power of ICT to produce the 'learning society'. The findings are rich and detailed, and include extracts from interviews with users and non-users of ICT. The overview and summary chapters are particularly valuable.

The results contradict much of the hype about the transforming potential of ICT and show in fact that ICT merely reinforces existing patterns of learning in adults. Those who are motivated, want to keep abreast of modern innovations or want to update their employment skills, now turn to ICT to accomplish this, whereas they would have used other means before the advent of ICT. The main barriers to adults learning after the mandatory school age are lack of interest and motivation, not lack of access to ICT. Furthermore, the authors found no indication that ICT made any impact on adults' motivation to learn. 'In short, the overriding message from our data is that there is little "special" or "new" about adult learning in the digital age (p. 174)'.

The findings showed that just over half of their sample made actual use of computers and the internet, though more than that had access.

The data confirms other studies in concluding that the use of computers and the internet is strongly associated with social class, education and location, indigeneity and birthplace (p. 76). The authors investigate the issue of informal learning, particularly in relation to learning to use a computer. They show evidence of the way in which this learning takes place over a long period of time, with many inputs from family, friends, colleagues and occasionally formal courses.

This large-scale study of adults' learning propensities is undoubtedly a valuable addition to the literature. It is also salutary to probe beneath the elearning bandwagon, to see the real place of learning in peoples' lives. This book is a good antidote to the overselling of elearning, and provides a vivid and research-based picture of the barriers to elearning. However, in focusing on the 50 per cent of adults who are not lifelong learners, the authors downplay the importance of the 50 per cent who are! Is the ICT glass half empty or half full?

Oblinger, D. and Oblinger, J. (eds)(2005). *Educating the Net Generation*. EDUCAUSE Publication. Available as a free pdf download at: http://www.educause.edu/books/educatingthenetgen/5989

This 'book' is the opposite in just about every way to the adult learners book described above: it is an edited collection of relatively short chapters; it concerns the generation born since 1983 that has grown up with computers; it is only available electronically and has an associated website with additional resources such as video clips. The fifteen chapters attempt to explain the thinking, behaviours and learning habits of this so-called Net Generation ('Net Gen'), and to consider the implications for educational institutions. Three generations: Baby Boomers (born 1946–1964), Gen X (1965–1982) Net Gen (1983–1991) are distinguished, but age is not the only defining characteristic. The technologies with which the user engages regularly and the attitude of mind towards information technology both contribute to Net Gen approaches to teaching and learning.

Three of the chapters are by Net Generation students, who describe their preoccupation with computer games, with mobile communication devices, with Instant Messaging and with customisation of technologies. In relation to education, they emphasise the importance of interactivity and learning by doing, and they indicate an expectation that professors will use technology to better communicate expert knowledge.

Surprisingly, what emerges from the surveys of 'Net Geners', is that the technology is not important; it is the activity which it enables that features most strongly for them. Similarly, they are not particularly concerned with what media are used by their instructors; they are more concerned with how well their lecturers convey their knowledge and subject expertise.

The chapters by academics and administrators address issues about how education needs to adapt to the changing requirements of the Net Generation. First of all, the curriculum and particularly assessment need to be re-thought. The Net Generation values experiential learning, working in teams, and social networking, and all of these have implications for the traditional lecture. One chapter outlines different types of interaction (for example, people-to-people, people and tools, people with concepts), and provides examples of projects that put these interactions into practice.

If the curriculum needs to change, it follows that faculty will need staff development in order to understand the changes and be able to adapt their teaching content and methods. Student services also need to alter, as do the library and the learning spaces on campus. Different chapters address these issues.

The final chapter considers the way in which immersive environments can be used to enhance learning and discusses the effects of the new media on the learning styles of the Net Generation.

A number of the chapters contain the results of surveys e.g. about the technologies students have, about their views on interaction and instructor support, and some are based on research. But the tone of the book is largely anecdotal and the writing style is very accessible. The perspective is wholly American and some of the chapters attempt the risky business of predicting the nature of the university in the future, or at least the technologies students will be using. We have chosen this book for this list because, as the editors say in their introduction, it is:

> a book for educators. Those who have chosen to be educators are generally dedicated to students. But, sometimes we don't quite understand what we are seeing. We hope this book will help educators make sense of the many patterns and behaviors that we see in the Net Generation but don't quite understand.

Naidu, S. (ed.)(2003). *Learning & Teaching with Technology: Principles and practices.* **London and New York: RoutledgeFalmer.**

The majority of contributors to this book are from Australian universities and the rest are from New Zealand, North America and Europe. As the title suggests, the focus of the nineteen chapters is the use of technology in teaching, and hence blended learning, rather than fully online learning, is the primary practice discussed by most of the authors. The editor has aimed to produce a book about the core processes of the teaching and learning transaction, rather than a collection of case studies.

Part One of the book concerns the use of technology to represent subject matter content. However, the focus of the four chapters in Part One is not on the representation of facts, principles or procedures, but on using technology to create environments in which learners can come to understand and gain insights into the subject. For example, one chapter articulates a set of guidelines for presenting domain knowledge by guiding the process of multimedia object selection, navigational objects selection and integration of multimedia objects to suit different learner needs.

Part Two focuses on the activation of learning and student engagement with content. The technologies used include simulations, photographs, shockwave movies and Quicktime video clips. Teacher education, medical education, cultural studies and social work are the subject areas to which the technology is applied.

Communication is the focus of the third part, and the authors consider technology supports for interaction and socialisation. Cooperative and collaborative strategies are considered, as well as asynchronous online discussions. The chapter on second language learning is particularly notable in its exploration of the role of online networking, web-based projects and the negotiation of meaning through textual interaction.

Technology support for assessment of learners is the subject of the fourth part of the book. Eportfolios, collaborative assignments and online problem-solving are all considered. The principles underlying the use of technology in assessment include the need to assess process as part of the learning outcomes as well as content. The authors in this section suggest that ICT can enable the assessment of motivational, affective and meta-cognitive aspects of learning.

The book concludes with three chapters about the provision of feedback to students. The three types of feedback are considered: the obvious 'tutor to student', the technology-mediated 'content to student' and finally 'student to student'. Various methods for providing feedback to students at a distance are the focus of the last chapter; these include: distributing selected exemplars, using web-based forms and designing peer feedback as one of the assessment components.

The book concludes with a very thoughtful final commentary, highlighting the principles to emerge from the chapters. One of these is the role of the teacher in the ICT-based environment: the teacher becomes part of a design team by which the online component of the content is created; the teacher also makes a major (though not the only) contribution to providing feedback to learners. Another factor highlighted in the commentary is the support needed by students as they adapt to the learner-centred rather than teacher-centred approach of open-ended online environments.

The book has an extensive index which is always useful in an edited collection. It also has an introduction by the editor, which not only provides a synopsis of each chapter, but in addition outlines some of the principles relevant to each of the five topics.

Higgison, C. (ed.)(2000). *Online Tutoring e-Book.* **Heriot-Watt University, Edinburgh. Available only online: http:// otis.scotcit.ac.uk/onlinebook**

This is a very practical and accessible book with a global reach. It consists of nine chapters and sixty-five peer reviewed case studies submitted by online educators from all around the world. An e-workshop and online asynchronous discussion began the process and papers from the keynote speakers are also included in the book. Finally, a set of 329 papers and other resources are provided, along with a search facility to find relevant topics. The only limitation of this excellent ebook is that it is now somewhat dated.

The nine chapters have all been written for the web, as the example of chapter six on culture and ethics (Figure 10) indicates.

In addition to culture and ethics, the chapters cover: online learning,

6 Culture and Ethics

Michel Labour, Charles Juwah, Nancy White and Sarah Tolley

e-book Contents

6 Culture and Ethics

Executive

Summary

Download this

chapter (PDF)

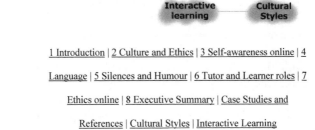

Figure 10 Chapter Six, Online Tutoring eBook

the tutor's role, building a community, assessment, evaluation, institutional support, staff development and quality assurance. The chapters draw on the tips, advice and experience of the practitioners as revealed in the online discussions and case studies, and in the process of writing a coherent chapter, the authors refer to other literature as well. The result is that each topic is a very rich resource in both breadth and depth.

The case studies can be grouped into the same nine themes as the book chapters or searched by category or author. They have been edited to provide the same fields for each one, which helps the reader to quickly understand the context of the case. While the book chapters discuss enduring issues, the case studies are more dated. Nevertheless, there are many issues that are still current, as this extract from a New Zealand case study on teacher education indicates:

> The lecturer set a series of weekly tasks throughout the semester that contributed to the development of the final piece of work. These tasks contributed to the design of a series of web pages about course related topics that the groups developed and then published as one linked site for each group. Some of the results were quite stunning – both in academic and in design terms. What was learnt? Perhaps most important was the need to ensure that groups were setting roles for each of their members so that all members were always involved in the weekly tasks. Maintaining the group cohesion over the semester was the most difficult part and within that, convincing the groups that they needed to be flexible enough to cut each other a bit of slack from time to time when pressures grew.

One of the keynote addresses is by the Australian Ruth Dunkin at RMIT, who, as Deputy Vice Chancellor, provides an institutional perspective on academic staff development. She considers the way in which elearning affects every aspect of the university and in particular, the change for academics from lecturing to course development through team work.

Another keynote address is by Palloff and Pratt who draw on extracts from their award-winning book, *Building Learning Communities in Cyberspace*. They address the following issues: ensuring access to and familiarity with the technology in use; establishing guidelines and procedures which are relatively loose and free-flowing, and generated with significant input from participants; striving to achieve maximum participation and 'buy-in' from the participants; promoting collaborative learning; and creating a double or triple loop in the learning process to enable participants to reflect on their learning process.

Bates, A. (2005). *Technology, E-Learning and Distance Education.*
London and New York: Routledge Taylor & Francis Group.

This is a fully updated version of Bates' 1995 edition, entitled *Technology, Open Learning and Distance Education.* Bates is a very well-known author in this field and a deservedly respected analyst and practitioner of distance education. In his Preface to this second edition he comments ruefully on the change of title (substituting ELearning for Open Learning), noting that distance education since 1995 has become less about open access and more about the commercialisation of elearning. He claims that distance education and elearning are different concepts though they have many synergies. Given his history of distance education experience, this view is not surprising; similarly, his statement:

> I have resisted the post-modernist tendency to believe that everything new is good and that there are no lessons to be learned from the past. Indeed, I believe quite the opposite. There are many useful lessons from the past that apply with as much force to new education technology development, and we ignore those lessons at our peril. (Preface to the Second Edition)

One of Bates' areas of expertise is in the costing of various learning technologies. In this edition, Bates adds web-based costings to his original costing chapters on print, television and radio. He also adds a chapter on synchronous interaction via the web, and compares this with audio and video conferencing.

Bates' new chapter entitled 'The impact of technology on the organisation of distance education', provides an overview of institutions worldwide that teach at a distance: the dual mode universities, the virtual universities, the for-profit ventures and partnerships and consortia. He looks at size, diversity and failure, and he notes that the web has transformed not only the pedagogy but also the organisational structures of distance education.

One of the terms for which Bates is famous, is his 'Lone Ranger' depiction of early adopter academics who work individually on creating their own web-based materials. This model is contrasted with 'Boutique course development' made up of a small support team operating 'on demand', meeting the specific needs of one academic wanting to put materials online. Finally, he identifies the collegial team development method in which online materials are developed collaboratively. While this depiction of course development methods may still have some relevance, on the whole the proliferation of VLEs has made the process of putting materials online easy enough for any academic, and the reliance on templates has drastically reduced the design requirements of online presentation.

The chapter on synchronous communication technologies takes the reader through audioconferencing, telephone-based videoconferencing, web-conferencing and broadband videoconferencing. Five modes of use are described: individual to individual (usually a teacher communicating with a single student), individual to group (usually an instructor to a single, remote group of students), instructor to remote individuals (usually to single students at individual sites), instructor to multiple groups (often used to deliver lectures to distributed campuses) and finally student to student groups in which students communicate with each other to work on projects or for self-help.

The author concludes:

> Neither distance education nor e-learning are panaceas, but the technology is now at a stage where we can teach in a wide variety of ways. The challenge is to move beyond arguments about technology, distance and time, to focusing on the needs of learners, and the most cost-effective ways to meet those needs. (p. 225)

This book is richly based on research, common sense and a vast knowledge and experience of both the history and the current state of elearning.

Journal articles

Brown, R. (2001). The process of community-building in distance learning classes, *JALN,* **5 (2) Available at: http:// www.sloan-c.org/publications/jaln/v5n2/index.asp**

This is a classic research study of the development of online community in an educational setting. It uses grounded theory methodology to analyse messages and includes interviews with students and faculty on three graduate level courses taught at a distance.

The author identified three levels of community, and each level involved a greater degree of engagement. Furthermore, an increased sense of community was associated with increased engagement in the class.

The three levels, perhaps predictably, are:

1. Development of a network of friends. Students communicated regularly with other students when they found something in common, be that academic, personal or geographic. Even this first level of community only happens if students actively seek it, and the 'lone learners' tend to avoid participation, or remain on the fringes.
2. Community of learners. This level of community was associated with long, thoughtful, threaded discussions on relevant subjects. Students found the experience of this kind of interaction personally satisfying and it created a sense of kinship amongst the participants. Membership in this kind of community was not based on personality but on the quality of the participant's input to the discussions.
3. Growth of camaraderie. This developed through personal communication, often over a long time or intense association, usually over several classes together. Significantly, it often involved face-to-face meetings.

The author goes on to define fifteen processes in the development of community which she explains in detail and then illustrates graphically. One of the processes is the issue of trust and earning the respect of fellow students.

> Earning each other's trust was a continuing effort that anchored a virtual friendship or even an acquaintance in the classroom community. This involved students continually demonstrating both their ability and their reliability: they consistently interacted positively with well-written, knowledgeable, timely, supportive input. (Brown, 2001: 29)

Brown has interesting findings regarding the issue of time allotted to the online discussions by students. She found that students who were comfortable with text-based communication tended to allot more time to the discussions and did not resent this extra time. Those who preferred oral communication and face-to-face interaction found the time demands of online discussion frustrating, both the time it took to write messages and the time it took to get responses.

The author draws on the student interview data to suggest ways in which the instructor can foster participation by distance learners and considers the learning benefits when students feel part of an online community.

Hedberg, J. and Lim, C. P. (2004). Charting trends for e-learning in Asian schools, *Distance Education*, 25 (2) 199–213.

These two authors are from the Nanyang Technological University in Singapore, which, like South Korea, is classed by UNESCO as an advanced country in terms of ICT infrastructure. In this article, the authors discuss elearning trends and challenges for universities and schools in both ICT developed and developing countries.

One trend the authors discuss is a move away from computer training as a separate subject, to an integrated approach where the computer is used as a tool for decision making, critical thinking and communication skills. Another trend involves partnerships with industry to develop multimedia, interactive materials, e.g. in physics. South Korea has identified an urgent need for education reform to meet the demands of a knowledge-based society. This has led to the development of digital libraries which facilitate greater freedom of choice in the time and place of learning. More significantly, the use of digital resources supports the social construction of knowledge by learners and a move away from passive, teacher-centred pedagogy.

The authors also consider developments in approaches to assessment in a number of countries as they respond to the curriculum changes brought about by ICT. Formative assessment is one innovation being used in Singapore, Thai and Indian schools. Different modes of assessment such as project work, interactive software and self-assessment are all being explored in Singapore, and in Thailand, authentic assessment, portfolio assessment, peer evaluation and performance assessment are part of the change process.

One of the elearning challenges presented by the authors is the need for a re-alignment of practice, policy and technology. To this end, they have developed a table in which they summarise the traditional and re-thought approaches. From this they identify three critically important issues:

- design of learning tasks;
- learning support and resources;
- communication methods.

Under the design issue, they consider authenticity, just-in-time learning and assessment. Under the support and resources issue, they discuss learning objects, knowledge management and digital libraries. Under communication methods, they consider communities of practitioners and emerging technologies.

They conclude:

> Thus, the real skill of modern teaching becomes the agility with which each teacher and student can weave into the learning environment these new resources and the insights that other people and places can provide. As the technology also subtly changes the nature of processes and the actual content of the curriculum, emerging technologies can be employed to support more elaborate assessments of processes and the creation of artefacts which demonstrate higher order thinking and reflection on the outcomes. (Hedberg and Lim, 2004: 210)

Rovai, A. (2004). A constructivist approach to online college learning, *The Internet and Higher Education,* **7, 79–93.**

Rovai is a prolific writer on the subject of online learning. In this particular article, he applies the principles of constructivism to online pedagogy. His aim is to summarise and also to contribute to the literature on good online course design. He presents a pragmatic view of constructivism as the 'product of many learner-centred processes'. There are a number of implications of constructivism for online learning: that the curriculum must be customised to the students' prior knowledge; the teaching strategies must be tailored to students' responses; open-ended questioning should be used so that students can be helped to construct meaning. He quotes Jonassen's guidelines on how to design constructivist online courses:

> Focus on knowledge construction, not reproduction . . . Present authentic tasks . . . [that] provide real world case-based learning environments . . . Foster reflective practice, and enable context and content dependent knowledge construction . . . Support collaborative construction of knowledge through social negotiation, not competition among learners for recognition. (Jonassen, 1994: 35)

Rovai's ideas on the presentation of content seem to be heavily influenced by a template model typical of commercial VLEs, and perhaps also by the American week-by-week modular structure. Similarly, his suggested rubric for superior course participation is that the student posts three or more constructive messages each calendar week, spread through the week. This inflexibility in course design leaves little room for the unforeseen family or workplace demands that are an inevitable part of most adults' lives.

The section on individual and group activities is particularly good. He recommends discouraging dependency on the instructor through a careful balance of individual work, class discussions, group work and interventions by the tutor to trigger self reflection. He also places great emphasis on grading students' contributions to online discussions, and gives evidence that this improves online discussion and development of community.

Assessment, he suggests, should be a combination of grading online contributions to discussions, tests, portfolios, individual and group projects and performances. Regarding the problem of plagiarism, he refers to Vrasidas and Glass (2002) who suggest four strategies to combat plagiarism by designing assessments in which:

1. Students use their own experiences.
2. Students have to apply course ideas to their own or at least to real-world contexts.
3. Students work collaboratively.
4. Students negotiate the assessment process with the instructor.

Rovai concludes the article with a list of the questions which we still need to research regarding the application of constructivist activities in online learning environments. For example, he notes that some activities are more effective than others, but we know little about why. Likewise, research is needed to identify the constructivist activities which result in higher order thinking skills.

In this article, Rovai appears to use the term distance education to mean elearning. 'Teaching at a distance is not just about using technology, it is also about perfecting a pedagogical art for effective online learning' (p. 90).

References

Jonassen, D. (1994). *Computers in Schools: Mindtools for Critical Thinking.* University Park, PA: Pennsylvania State University Press.

Vrasidas, C. and Glass, G. (2002). *Distance Education and Distributed Learning.* Greenwich, CT: Information Age Publishing.

McConnell, D. (2002). Action Research and Distributed Problem-Based Learning in Continuing Professional Education, *Distance Education,* **23 (1), 59–83.**

Problem-based learning is a course design approach that is particularly adaptable to the online environment. In this article, McConnell presents his research into the processes which distributed groups use when working collaboratively on problems. As the students in question are adult professionals, the approach taken by McConnell was not to present the groups with problems, but rather to allow each small elearning group to negotiate amongst themselves the focus of the problem they wished to tackle.

The methodology used in the two studies that form the substance of the article involved the author in observation, ethnography, textual analysis and in-depth interviews. His aim in the first study was to examine the way in which one distributed group negotiated the problem. In the second study he considers how the work undertaken by the group came to develop and sustain them as a learning community.

The masters level course which was the subject of the study was designed for elearning professionals and emphasised:

> the implementation of innovatory online practice by creating a supportive and creative research learning community where participants feel free to experiment and 'learn by doing', while constantly holding a critical perspective on their practice and the theory underpinning it. (McConnell, 2002: 61)

McConnell identified three phases in the development of the group:

- a long negotiating phase;
- a phase where the work is divided and the research for the problem is carried out;
- a third production phase.

He acknowledges that the phases are not discreet; there is movement forward and backward as the group begins to make sense of who they are and what the process and product of the problem is to be. As support for his findings, he presents a wide range of extracts both from the online interactions and from the interviews. His purpose in conveying this sense of group development is that it should be helpful to the practice of other tutors as they try to facilitate online group work:

Research of this kind – open-ended, exploratory, descriptive, grounded in real learning situations and contexts, addressing both broad themes and micro issues – helps us understand the complexity of learning and teaching in dPBL [distributed problem-based learning] environments and offers insights which can be useful in developing our practice. (McConnell, 2002: 80)

Shelton, K. and Saltsman, G. (2004). Tips and tricks for teaching online: How to teach like a pro!, *Instructional Technology and Distance Learning,* **1 (10) http://itdl.org/Journal/Oct_04/ article04.htm**

This article is unabashedly a how-to guide for online teaching. The tone is informal and the advice is geared to American higher education: short semesters, short learning modules and student participation requirements. Nevertheless, many of the practices suggested have universal relevance:

> The learning community, like a garden, must be cultivated. This cultivation occurs when an instructor provides ample communication, facilitates the discussion board, treats each student as an individual, adds emotion and belonging, responds quickly to questions, models required behavior, creates appropriately sized groups, and clearly outlines expectations for group activities.

The authors recommend that teachers focus a good deal of their communication at the beginning of a course, but gradually encourage students to take on some of this role as the course progresses. This letting go of control is something the authors recognise will be difficult for some faculty members who are used to dominating the learning environment through lecturing.

Several websites are identified that contain ideas for initial activities to generate discussion and hence alleviate students' nervousness about contributing to an online forum.

Another useful tip is that summaries by the teacher help to bring closure to modules and reminders of project and exam dates reduce individual queries. The authors suggest that teachers can assign the role of summarising discussions to particular students, as a way of increasing student involvement.

The issue of bringing emotion into the online discussions is addressed in this article, as it is by many other authors and researchers concerned with elearning. By establishing a warm and friendly tone, the online tutor can help students overcome the lack of visual clues and dispel feelings of loneliness that distance students often experience. Emoticons are one way of conveying emotion, but a more important principle is for the teacher to maintain an awareness of each student as an individual.

BIBLIOGRAPHY

Allen, I. and Seaman, J. (2004). *Entering the mainstream: The quality and extent of online education in the United States, 2003 and 2004.* Needham and Wellesley, MA: The Sloan Consortium.

Bangert, A. (2004). The seven principles of good practice: a framework for evaluating on-line teaching. *The Internet and Higher Education,* 7(3), 217–232.

Barbian, J. (2002). Blended Works: Here's Proof! *Online Learning,* 6(6), 26–31.

Bates, A. (2005). *Technology, E-Learning and Distance Education.* London and New York: Routledge Taylor & Francis Group.

Belanger, Y. (2005). Duke University iPod First Year Experience Final Evaluation Report, Duke University. Available at: http://cit.duke.edu/pdf/ipod_initiative_04_05.pdf

Boud, D. (1981). *Developing Student Autonomy in Learning* (2nd edition). London: Kogan Page.

Brown, R. (2001). The Process of Community-Building in Distance Learning Courses, *JALN,* 5(2).

Chambers, J. (1999). Speech at COMDEX. http://www.mercurycenter.com/archives/reprints/0300/killer_aps11191999.htm

Collis, B., De Boer, W. and Ven der Veen, J. (2002). Building on learner contributions: A Web-supported pedagogic strategy, *Educational Media International* 38(4), 229–240.

Coomey, M. and Stephenson, J. (2001). Online learning: It is all about dialogue, involvement, support and control – according to research. In: *Teaching and Learning Online. Pedagogies for New Technologies* (ed. J. Stephenson). London: Kogan Page.

Cross, J. (n.d.) Available at: http://www.jaycross.com/#aboutjay

Eklund, J., Kay, M. and Lynch, H. (2003) E-learning: emerging issues and key trends. Australian Flexible Learning Framework Discussion Paper. Available at: www.flexiblelearning.net.au

Ewell, P. (1997). Organizing for learning. A new imperative. *AAHE Bulletin,* American Association for Higher Education. Available online: http://aahebulletin.com/member/articles/organizingewell.asp?pf=1

Guri-Rosenblit, S. (2005). Eight paradoxes in the implementation process of e-learning in higher education, *Higher Education Policy* 18, 5–29. Available at: http://www.palgrave-journals.com/cgi-taf/DynaPage.taf?file=/hep/journal/v18/n1/full/8300069a.html&filetype=pdf

Harasim, L. (ed.) (1990). *Online Education: Perspectives on a New Environment.* New York: Praeger Publishers.

Hildreth, P. and Kimble, C. (2002). The duality of knowledge, *Information Research*, 8(1). Available at: http://informationr.net/ir/8–1/paper142.html

Hisham, N., Campton, P. and FitzGerald, D. (2004). A tale of two cities: A study on the satisfaction of asynchronous e-learning systems in two Australian universities, *ASCILITE Conference Proceedings*, Perth. Available at: http://www.ascilite.org.au/conferences/perth04/procs/hisham.html

Jackson, S. (2004). Ahead of the curve: future shifts in higher education, *Educause*, January/February.

Jarvenpaa, S., Knoll, K. and Leidner, D. (1998). Is anybody out there? Antecedents of trust in global virtual teams, *Journal of Management Information Systems*, 14(4), 29–64.

Jones, S. and Madden, M. (2002). The Internet goes to college, *Pew Internet Report* 71. Available at: http://www.pewInternet.org/PPF/r/71/report_display.asp

Jones, S. and Johnson-Yale, Community (2005). Professors online: The Internet's impact on college faculty, *First Monday*, 10/9. Available at: http://firstmonday.org/issue10_9/jones/index.html

Lave, J. and Wenger, E. (1990). *Situated Learning: Legitimate Peripheral Participation*. Cambridge, UK: Cambridge University Press.

McConnell, D. (2002). The experience of collaborative assessment in e-learning, *Studies in Continuing Education*, 24(1), 73–92.

Mason, R. (2000). IET's Masters in Open and Distance Education. What have we learned? http://iet.open.ac.uk/pp/r.d.mason/downloads/maeval.pdf

Mason, R., Pegler, C. and Weller, M. (2005). A learning object success story *JALN*, 9(1), March.

Mayes, T. (2002). Pedagogy, lifelong learning and ICT: A discussion paper for the Scottish Forum on Lifelong Learning. Available at: http://www.usq.edu.au/electpub/e-jist/docs/html2002/pdf/mayes.pdf

Meng, P. (2005). Podcasting and vodcasting – definitions, discussions and implications. A White Paper, University of Missouri. Available at: http://edmarketing.apple.com/adcinstitute/wp-content/Missouri_Podcasting_White_Paper.pdf

Merriam, S. and Caffarella, R. (1999). *Learning in Adulthood* (2nd edn) San Francisco: Jossey-Bass.

O'Neill, K. Singh, G. and O'Donoghue, J., (2004) Implementing elearning programmes for higher education: a review of the literature, *Journal of Information Technology Education*, 3, available at http://jite.org/documents/Vol3/v3p313–323–131.pdf

Preston, D. (2004). *Virtual Learning and Higher Education*. Rodopi: Amsterdam.

Rennie, F. and Mason, R. (2004). *The Connecticon: Learning for the Connected Generation*. USA: Information Age Publishing.

Reynolds, J., Caley, L. and Mason, R. (2002). How do people learn? Chartered Institute of personnel and development research report. Available at: http://www.cipd.co.uk/publications

Rosenberg, M. (2001). *e-Learning: Strategies for Delivering Knowledge in the Digital Age*, New York: McGraw-Hill.

Rovai, A. (2001). Building classroom community at a distance: A case study, *Educational Technology Research and Development Journal*, 49(4), 33–48.

Rovai, A. and Jordan, H. (2004). Blended learning and sense of community: a comparative analysis with traditional and fully online graduate courses, *IRRODL*, 5(2) Available at: www.irrodl.org/content/v5.2/rovai-jordan.html

Salmon, G. (2002). *E-tivities: The key to active online learning*, London: RoutledgeFalmer.

Slavin, R. (1994). Student teams-achievement divisions. In: *Handbook of Cooperative Learning* (ed. S. Sharan), pp. 3–19, Westport, CT: Greenwood Press.

Stacey, E. (1998). Learning collaboratively in a CMC environment. In: *Teleteaching 98: Distance Learning, Training and Education, Proceedings of the XV IFIP World Computer Congress* (ed. G. Davies), pp. 951–960, Vienna and Budapest: Austrian Computer Society (OCG).

Stephens, D. and Creaser, C. (2002). Information science student IT experience and attitude to computers: results of a five-year longitudinal study, *Italics*, 1(2). Available at: http://www.ics.ltsn.ac.uk/pub/italics/issue2/dstephens_b/005.html

Swan, K. (2003). Developing social presence in online course discussions. In: *Learning & Teaching with Technology: Principles and practices* (ed. S. Naidu). London: Taylor & Francis.

Thompson, M. (2004). Faculty self-study research project: examining the online workload, *JALN*, 8(3).

Wlodkowski, R. (1999). *Enhancing Adult Motivation to Learn* (revised edn.), San Francisco, CA: Jossey-Bass.

Wood, K. (2003). Introduction to mobile learning, Becta. Available at: http://ferl.becta.org.uk/display.cfm?page=65&catid=192&resid=5194&printable=1

Young, J. (2002). 'Hybrid' teaching seeks to end the divide between traditional and online instruction, *The Chronicle of Higher Education*, 48(28). Available at: http://chronicle.com/free/v48/i28/28a03301.htm

INDEX

Cyberculture: The Key Concepts

David Bell, Brian D. Loader, Nicholas Pleace and Douglas Schuler

This comprehensive A–Z guide provides a wide-ranging and up-to-date overview of the fast-changing and increasingly important world of cyberculture. Its clear and accessible entries cover aspects ranging from the technical to the theoretical, and from movies to the everyday, including:

- Artificial intelligence
- Cyberfeminism
- Cyberpunk
- Electronic government
- Games
- Hacktivists
- HTML
- *The Matrix*
- Netiquette
- Piracy.

Fully cross-referenced, easy to use and with suggestions for further reading, this is an essential resource for anyone interested in cyberculture.

0 415 24754 3 / 978 0 415 24754 2

Available at all good bookshops
For ordering and further information please visit
www.routledge.com

Related titles from Routledge

Primary Education
The Key Concepts
Denis Hayes

Written for students, practitioners and policy-makers, *Primary Education: The Key Concepts* is a clear and accessible guide to the most important ideas and issues involved in the education of children at this crucial and formative time in their lives.

Alphabetically arranged and fully cross-referenced to ensure ease of use, entries include both curriculum specific and generic theoretical terms, such as:

- Assessment
- Objectives
- Copying strategies
- Differentiation
- Behaviour
- Special needs
- Time management

Written by an experienced teacher and lecturer, *Primary Education: The Key Concepts* is a concise yet comprehensive text that takes into account the everyday realities of teaching. Readable and user-friendly, it is a first-class resource for the primary practitioner at all levels.

0–415–35483–8
978–0–415–35483–7

Available at all good bookshops
For ordering and further information please visit:
www.routledge.com

Related titles from Routledge

Secondary Education
The Key Concepts
Jerry Wellington

A comprehensive critical survey of the controversies, theories and practices central to secondary education today, this book provides teachers, researchers, parents and policy-makers alike with a vital new reference resource.

Secondary Education: The Key Concepts covers important topics, including:

- Assessment
- Citizenship
- Curriculum
- Elearning
- Exclusion
- Theories of learning
- Work experience

Fully cross-referenced, with extensive suggestions on further reading and on-line resources, *Secondary Education: The Key Concepts* is the essential guide to theory and practice in the twenty-first-century classroom.

0-415-34404-2
978-0-415-34404-3

Available at all good bookshops
For ordering and further information please visit:
www.routledge.com